Super Strategies
for Puzzles and Games

Super Strategies for Puzzles and Games

Saul X. Levmore
Elizabeth Early Cook

DOUBLEDAY & COMPANY, INC.
GARDEN CITY, NEW YORK
1981

Our thanks go to the following authors and publishers for allowing us to use examples from their challenging books.

Russell L. Ackoff, *The Art of Problem Solving,* copyright © 1978 by John Wiley & Sons, Inc. Reprinted by permission of John Wiley & Sons, Inc.

E. R. Emmet, *Brain Puzzler's Delight,* copyright © 1967, 1970 by E. R. Emmet. Reprinted by permission of Emerson Books, Inc.

L. H. Longley-Cook, *More Puzzle Fun,* copyright © 1977 by L. H. Longley-Cook. Reprinted by permission of Fawcett Books.

H. E. Dudeney's books, particularly *536 Puzzles and Curious Problems,* published by Charles Scribner's Sons, have also been a source of inspiration.

ISBN: 0-385-17165-X
Library of Congress Catalog Card Number 81–43275

To friends made at Yale

Acknowledgments

Grateful acknowledgment is made to all those associated with the Yale College Seminar Program and to the students on whom much of this material was first forced: Julie Abrahamson, Steven Baird, David Bowen, Stewart Hudson, George Langdon, Peter McCabe, Heather Meeker, Robert Nassau, Hillary Nelson, Naomi Rutenberg, Eric Saldinger, Steven Salzberg, Laura Scher, Fred Siegel, and many wonderful economics students who cheerfully put up with the occasional digressions from graphs.

In this group, particular credit is owed to Peter and Fred for contributions that appear in chapter 1, Naomi for work on the tactoe games, Hillary for the creation and presentation of Array, Laura for developing the basics of Barter, Julie for painstaking work on the predecessor of Secrets, David for the creation and execution of Circuit, and to Robert for the brainstorm of Hidden-Tac-Toe. The unintelligible words in this paragraph are the names of games that are described in chapter 3 and that we hope you will soon enjoy.

The greatest debt is owed to those friends and acquaintances who enjoyed sharing new puzzles, games, and ideas and to those teachers and students at Yale who particularly relished the idea that the lessons of games and puzzles are applicable to real-life problems. While it would be difficult to acknowledge all these individuals by name, special thanks go to Stuart Gross, Roslyn and Vivian Levmore, and to all those friends who often hated, but always tolerated, the time spent on these topics. Finally, I owe many thanks to my editor, Nan Grubbs, for her professionalism, humor, and encouragement.

S.L.

Contents

Introduction

Puzzles and games can be both fun and important. If you like desserts, for example, then at an early age you probably faced the problem of sharing one delicious portion with a competitive friend or sibling. How did you go about dividing that fantastic chocolate cake? A measuring tape is of little help because the creamy icing is usually the best part of the piece. A long time ago, someone's parents seem to have solved this problem, assuring themselves that neither child would burst into tears after the division was completed and complain that the other kid's piece was better. This solution could be called "you cut, I choose": Jill plots her move and then slices the cake knowing that she will be left with the piece that Jack does not select.

Is this a fair solution? It seems that Jack, who gets to choose among the alternative portions, has gotten the better deal. If Jill moves the knife unintentionally or lacks a good eye for these things, then Jack will grin and grab the bigger and better piece. The "chooser" can only be equal to or better off than the "cutter." It is much better to let the other person cut so that you retain your options.*

* On the other hand, in dividing up book collections or other things, it might be better to be the cutter. For example, you might know something about the likes and dislikes of the other person and be able to put a book or two in pile A to ensure that your competitor will choose that pile, saving all the books you cherish for pile B. If your competitor did the cutting, he might not consider your favorite books—unless you tell him—and could split them up by chance. In short, at times the cutter, like an agenda-setter, enjoys great power in his ability to limit other people's options.

Super Strategies for Puzzles and Games will lead you through all
kinds of puzzles and games and teach you which questions to ask
and which strategies to develop. The "you cut, I choose" solution
that you have just seen is typical of many in this book as it is applicable to a variety of subjects other than good chocolate cake. After
all, business partners need a way to divide up their assets and
families may also need to split up and go their separate ways.

Could this strategy be extended to three or four partners or siblings? Indeed, this is a very difficult question and one that you
might think about before meeting again later in the book.

The enthusiasm generated by a Yale College seminar that Saul
taught in 1978 was the original stimulus for this book. The seminar
was entitled "Construction and Analysis of Games and Puzzles"
and the 200 applicants for the course made it one of the most popular offerings at Yale. These students were interested not only in
winning games and solving puzzles but also in logical and thematic
analyses of some common elements that are found in games and
puzzles.

A puzzle, on its surface, is different from a game in that once a
puzzle is solved it cannot be played again the way a game can. But
really, no puzzle or game comes to an end. The lessons that are
learned in the solving and in the playing are often transferable to
other challenges. Throughout the semester, the seminar participants
saw that an idea used in solving one problem could be applied to
another, seemingly unrelated, puzzle. Often the correct strategy involved reducing a problem to simpler versions and then slowly
building it back up to include the elements that were originally
presented. At other times, more scientific methods were employed
in order to avoid the frustration of trial-and-error approaches. The
class began to understand how the construction of a puzzle might
lead the reader's mind away from the correct strategy and solution.

The analysis of most games proved to be a more difficult enter-
prise, however. As the weeks went by, we did find that similar elements appear in a variety of games and that a comprehension of
the underlying structures can make for more fun and challenge. In
some games, elements of randomness were incorporated, board sizes
were changed, and other components such as risks, goals, and order
of play were varied. The class finished the semester by constructing

new games—a task that called upon the powers of analysis and ingenuity, which had increased from working with games and puzzles over a substantial period of time.

Various versions of old and new puzzles are contained in the following pages. Some have been worked through to their solutions with much detail, and others are solved and accompanied by a discussion of why the strategy that at first *seemed* obvious did not, in fact, get you very far. Some puzzles, of course, have been left to the reader in order to see if he can apply the theories of analysis that were presented in earlier examples.

In addition to puzzles, the material in this book deals with board games, card games, word games, and weird games, some of which —but not many of which—are likely to be familiar. Some of the more familiar games have been altered to make them more fun while others are more carefully explained so that a player can structure his own winning strategy using the analysis we provide.

Finally, the most exciting part of the book contains new and very original games that you can play, teach, and modify, if you like. We have given you complete rules for setting up the games as well as analyses of how the games are best attacked and played. It is our hope that these ideas will, in turn, give *you* ideas for constructing your own new games and that you'll send us a copy so we can try them out!

When you are able to understand what a game or puzzle is asking and when you can consistently arrive at a rational strategy for winning or solving, then you will understand what is meant by "thematic approaches to games and puzzles." Your strategic ability will be useful, satisfying, and enjoyable. Most approaches will involve some scientific method, a bit of logical reasoning, and the knowledge that there *are* familiar themes that can be uncovered. We have had a great deal of fun with games and puzzles and we hope that this book will allow you to do the same. Enjoy!

Super Strategies
for Puzzles and Games

1

Thematic Approaches

It is now time to begin making you an expert at seeing through and solving puzzles—and enjoying yourself at the same time. Chapter 1 is full of puzzles of all kinds and all difficulties. To help you measure your progress, each puzzle is numbered in terms of how hard it is to solve. A "1" is fairly easy and a "5" is very difficult. Be forewarned that these problems are very challenging, so any step in the direction of the correct solution deserves some applause. Now dig in!

When someone mentions expansion, what comes to your mind? A river rising to fill its bed? The aftermath of a good meal? Expansion can be unlimited, but it can also take place within certain boundaries or in only one direction at a time. When the idea of expansion is applied to puzzles, it means that the components of the puzzle are exaggerated in some way. It is a technique that helps to solve some puzzles because the enlarged factors highlight the essence of the problem's real identity. Here's an example of how expanding a puzzle can help you see a solution.

THE BRIDGE PROBLEM
Difficulty: 3 (without paper); 2 (with paper and pen)

Four men must cross a bridge over a deep ravine in enemy territory in the middle of the night. The treacherous bridge will hold only two men at once and it is necessary to carry a lantern while crossing. One of the men takes 5 minutes for the trip across, one takes 10, a third man requires 20, and the last needs 25 minutes. Unfortunately, they have only one lantern among them. How can they make it across if they have only 60 minutes before the bridge is blown up?

This is a good problem with a good answer, and to keep you on the right track, here is a list of several possible answers that, although clever, are not correct. The men do *not* throw the lantern back and forth across the bridge; this would create a new problem in which the total crossing time would be 35 minutes. Perhaps you should assume that the bridge has a surface that is buckling, because the men also do not roll the lantern across. Nor does one large man juggle the smaller ones across the bridge (although juggling is a cute answer to the problem of the ninety-pound man who must, in one crossing, carry two ten-pound weights across a bridge with a capacity of one hundred pounds)!

Think about the Bridge Problem and work on it for a while. Even if you think you have found the answer, do not skip over the explanation that follows (or any others in this chapter), because understanding this answer will help you work out some of the other problems coming up.

(The blank spaces throughout the book are meant to keep you from looking at the answer immediately after having read the problem. You might use these spaces for your own work although many of these problems are more enjoyable if tackled only in the mind.)

The most obvious way to attack this problem is to begin with trial-and-error attempts. It is possible to hit on the right solution this way, but it makes for slow work and it's just as likely that you will continue to come up with combinations that require more than sixty minutes. Now if you try *expanding* the problem you may see the crucial "trick" upon which the solution depends. Think of the same problem, but imagine now that the third man requires 1,000 minutes to cross and the fourth needs 1,005. (Since the men are still racing against the clock, they must cross the bridge in 1,040 minutes to stay alive.) Try to find a solution to this version of the problem. Does this change make you see something that you overlooked before? It should be clear that the two slow travelers *must* cross together because it would be an extravagant (and deadly) waste of time to make both the 5- and 10-minute travelers dawdle across the bridge with a lethargic compatriot.

Bringing this insight back to the original problem should result in a solution quickly reached. Since the two slower men should cross the bridge together (and only once), the two quicker men must start by crossing together. This will absorb 10 minutes because they must adopt the pace of the slower of the two so that the lantern serves both. Since the lantern must return to the departure side of the ravine for the two slow men to use, one of the quicker men brings it back by himself. It can be either one, but assume the quickest man makes the trip, and another 5 minutes have passed. The two slow men leave immediately with the lantern, and their crossing lasts 25 minutes. The 10-minute man who was left alone on the new shore grabs the lantern and crosses the bridge (in 10 minutes) to pick up his buddy. They travel again across the ravine in 10 minutes, and the four men are united on the far shore just in time to hear the explosion and watch the bridge crumple and crumble.

With the solution just reached, it would seem appropriate for you to ask how you're supposed to know which elements in a puzzle to expand. In this bridge problem, you might have tried expanding the time the men had to cross the bridge, but that wouldn't show you a new approach to the problem, it would just simplify it. If you were curious during your first reading of the puzzle, you might have wondered why the men's crossing times were 5, 10, 20, and 25 instead of 5, 10, 15, and 20. The gap is important but can easily be overlooked as it's so small. Expanding the problem by increasing the two slower traveling times then highlights the time gap. With some experience and insight, the potential solver should realize that the four men are really divided into two groups, fast and slow, and that they must cross the bridge accordingly to avoid wasting time.

The point of applying the technique of expansion to a puzzle is to acquire a new perspective on the problem. Sometimes this technique, or any other like it, will give direct results and yield a solution. Often its virtue lies in merely jogging the mind away from a chain of thought that has been unsuccessful. Since a puzzle frequently will not relinquish its secret to a simple persistent effort, any approach that encourages the mind to bend a little and entertain new options for solutions must be valuable.

DOT PROBLEMS
Difficulty: 3

Now here's a puzzle that may already be familiar to you. You must connect these nine dots using only four straight lines, without lifting your pencil off the page (using a *pen* to make four lines does not constitute a solution).

        •   •   •

        •   •   •

        •   •   •

If you don't know the answer already, stop and work on it awhile. Use this space for a couple of tries (or several hours' worth) and then turn the page to see the answer.

The traditional answer to the nine-dot puzzle is revealed below:

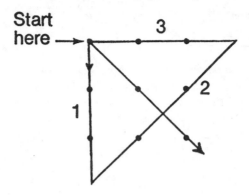

The figure below offers a less conventional solution that involves folding the paper so that one pencil line will connect two rows of dots at one time. The problem is then solved with three lines.

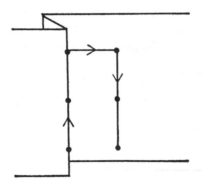

Both answers require that you step outside the bounds of a problem as you try to solve it, either literally, by making pencil lines that extend beyond the dots, or mentally, by thinking to fold the paper. Maybe now it doesn't seem so ridiculous that we excluded lantern-throwing as a solution to the bridge-crossing problem. If you are really letting your mind wander without inhibitions while searching for solutions, then throwing the lantern *should* occur to you, as should extended lines or folded paper. The kind of thinking that is not restrained by what appear to be the limits of a problem is more likely to discover a solution. Before you turn the pages of this book, however, you should have confidence that our solutions will be elegant. In other words, we will not resort to folding paper and throwing lanterns.

To see how easily one can learn to analyze puzzles, try the variation of the nine-dot puzzle that is presented below. These twenty-five dots must be connected by eight contiguous straight lines.

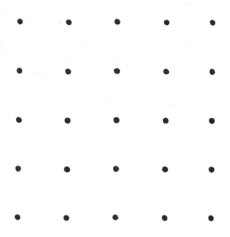

Spend some time with it and then turn for the answer.

Here it is:

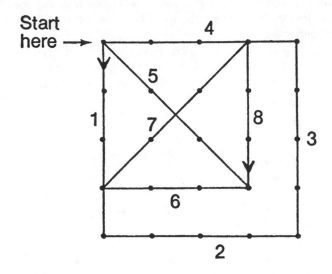

You might have come to this solution anyway, but if you're sharp today, this 5 by 5 problem should be easy. The trick to solving it is to reduce the grid to the form you're already familiar with, the 3 by 3. You do this by using your first four lines to trace the dots on the perimeter, leaving nine dots and four lines, which you have already mastered.

This method of reducing a puzzle to simpler elements in order to solve it is called *contraction*. It is generally more helpful than expansion in understanding puzzles because people find it easier to deal first with a simpler problem and then expand their comprehension to a harder problem when necessary.

If you need some more practice try out your new understanding of contraction theory on these two variations of the dot puzzle. The sixteen-dot puzzle uses six lines, and the twenty-dot uses seven.

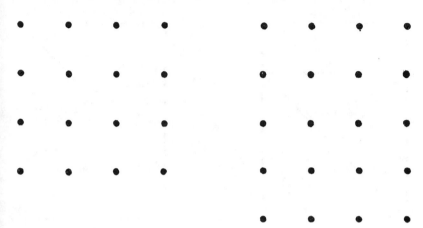

In both puzzles, as you probably saw right away, the trick again is to reduce the problem to nine dots and then solve with the familiar method.

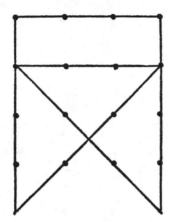 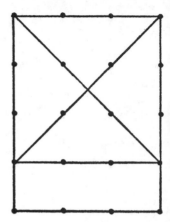

Are you ready for more complicated problems with these ridiculous dots? The insight you should have gained from reducing many-dot problems to the familiar nine-dot situation (3 by 3) will stand you in good stead. As demonstrated by the following examples, even renowned mathematicians are more likely to attempt new and ingenious proofs (with inferior results) than to utilize the possibilities of contraction. So if you're able to use contraction successfully, count yourself in an elite group.

As implied earlier, you often find problems asking you to connect X dots with Y straight lines. Try 4 by 3 dots with five lines. Here's a typical "book answer," suggested by L. H. Longley-Cook in one of his delightful books, *More Puzzle Fun.*

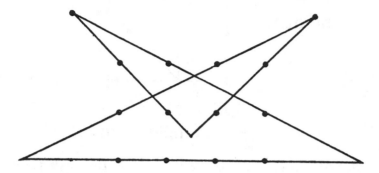

It doesn't look like a solution that would pop into your head quickly. The problem is much easier after step 1 in the figure below, which boils it down to our old friend.

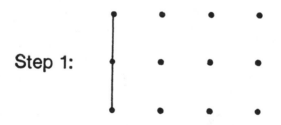

and then: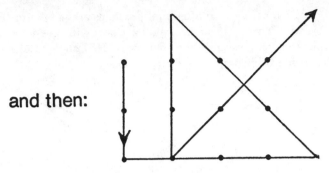

completes the job.

Similarly, here are two examples from H. E. Dudeney's *536 Puzzles and Curious Problems*. First you are asked to sink forty-nine (7 by 7) fishing boats in twelve straight courses.

It's an easy job, given our dot knowledge.

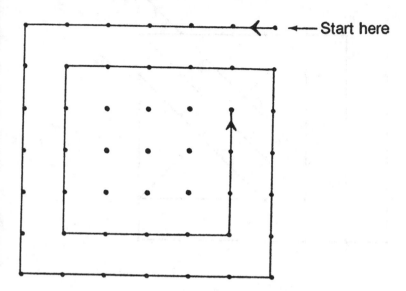

← ← Start here

After eight perimeter lines are drawn, the 3 by 3 problem is all that remains. It is possible that the problem will ask that the boat killer finishes at the starting point. Some inspection will show that our simple contraction procedure can let the boat killer out in a number of directions, but not so easily in the direction of the start. A little playing around might yield the following result, which subtly contains the same old theme.

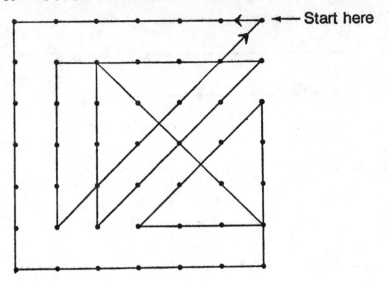

Start here

Here's another intriguing puzzle from Mr. Dudeney's book that gave us great satisfaction:

A traveler starts from the point marked below and wants to go 76 miles in 16 straight trips (lines) without retracing any part of his journey. The dots are towns—all one mile apart on the straight lines. You must show a route in which 76 miles are covered in 16 straight lines and only three towns are unvisited.

You should notice that contraction cannot start immediately because of the location of the starting point.

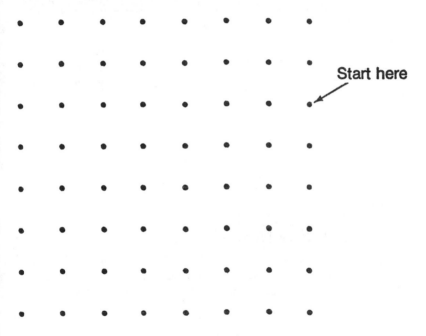

The book's solution is declared "not easy" and seems to require a great deal of trial and error.

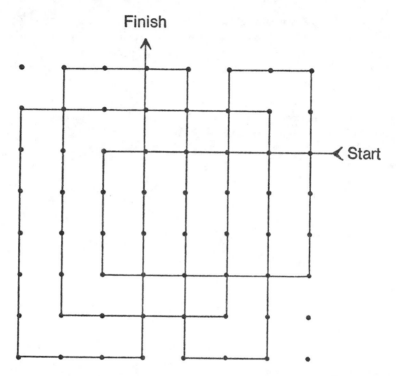

If you're a lazy reader, here are the miles traveled in the 16 steps above: $5 + 3 + 5 + 5 + 2 + 6 + 4 + 6 + 3 + 7 + 2 + 6 + 6 + 6 + 3 + 7 = 76$ miles. We are told that there is a 76-mile, 16-segment path that leaves just a single town unvisited. Give it a try.

Probably by now you're aching to try some contraction on this problem, and it really does work in a spectacular way:

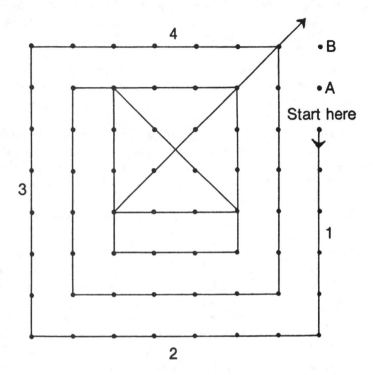

The starting spot might initially lead us to believe that we will solve the problem the familiar way and miss the town marked A, because we start by traveling toward the south for 5 miles. But after 10 steps we have the familiar 3 by 3 and after 14 steps the problem is completed. Towns A and B are still unvisited. We could now solve the problem literally by step 15 to town B, or improve on the answer by going through B to A as well, leaving *no* towns unvisited.

Presumably, you're worried about the 76-mile limit, so let's add up the distances: $5 + 7 + 7 + 6 + 6 + 5 + 5 + 4 + 4 + 3 + 4 + 3$ and a fraction (along the diagonal, so $3\sqrt{2}$ to be exact) $+ 3 + 5$ and a fraction ($5\sqrt{2}$) $+ 2$ (back to A). All this totals

69 plus fractions or approximately 72.312 miles. But we've used only 15 lines, so we can easily complete the problem by doing some sightseeing or driving off in a new direction for some miles! Better yet, of course, is to assume that the traveler wants to save miles and money so that visiting all the towns in fewer miles is a better answer.

It's probable that the original author of this puzzle did not consider the possibility of diagonal roads. Even if these roads don't exist, the time and gas that is saved seems to warrant building them!

Enough of dots, but please remember the powers of contraction and expansion. If a situation *looks* familiar, chances are that the principle behind the solution of a simple problem can be applied to the more difficult version at hand. Your best tool is your own power of inspection (assisted perhaps by contraction and . . .) and *not* a mathematical proof that comes to you without an intuitive feel.

Having discussed expansion and contraction theories as they are used in problem solving, it's time to add a third idea to the repertoire: *symmetry*. Symmetry is not as much a solving method as it is a component of many puzzles, and it is the simple recognition of this unannounced component that is so important. Often a puzzle's symmetry will be disguised to throw the solver off the track, or inversely, an apparent symmetry will be emphasized in order to make the solver *think* two very different situations are symmetrical. Looking closely to see if symmetry is really incorporated into a problem may be the first step to understanding and solving it. Consider this challenge:

THE SULTAN'S LAW
Difficulty: 3

In ancient Arabia, there was a sultan who believed that each man should marry more than one woman. Therefore, the sultan wanted to adjust the population of his country so that there were more women than men. He set down a law that required every couple to continue having children until it had its first boy and then to stop having children altogether.

How well did the sultan's plan work?

Once the law had been in effect for some years, what was the average family size?

Stop and work this out.

Your first reaction to this is probably that the sultan's scheme did work and that the number of females in the population increased with respect to the number of males. But this is incorrect. The puzzle implies an asymmetry that may have seduced you, namely that there exists *some* way of changing the natural ratio of men to women. What you must remember is the symmetry in childbirth, even though it is unstated in this problem. At every birth there is a 50 percent chance of having a boy and a 50 percent chance of having a girl. Keeping this in mind, do you come up with new answers?

Now work through the problem again. We know that all fertile, law-abiding women will have one child (call this the first "generation" of children). Of these, 50 percent will be boys and 50 percent, girls. The women who gave birth to boys stop having children and the other half of all mothers go on to have a second child. Of this second "generation," half are boys and half are girls. Only one quarter of all the country's mothers—those who had girls in the second "generation"—can continue on and have a third child. Again, in this third round, half the children are boys and half girls. This pattern continues, and it is always true that in each round, or "generation," half of all children born are boys and half are girls. The sultan's plan decreed the *number* of births for each mother but could not alter the natural ratio between the sexes. Only if some women really had a propensity to give birth to girls would the plan work.

Contraction is a good method to use when searching for the answer to the harder question which asked for the average family size in Sultanland. Instead of trying to calculate an average family size for the whole country, think about one sample family. Each family *must* have one boy (and then stop having children). Furthermore, for every boy there is one girl, since births are generally fifty-fifty. Therefore our "average" family has two children, one boy and one girl.

The answers to both questions really hinge on the fact of symmetrical birth ratios. One factor we didn't consider, however, was multiple births. How would our answers change if we included

twins and triplets in our calculations? What would happen if the
sultan banished women who broke his law?* Think about it.

---

* A thoughtful reader may consider mortality rates (higher for men,
especially in countries that war frequently and in which men go to work
more than women). Additionally, males *are* actually born in slightly more
than 50 percent of all childbirths. A curious fact! But we can ignore all
this for the problem's sake.

Here are a few problems that provide examples of symmetry and asymmetry. This first one might even help you win a little extra money sometime.

HEADS AND TAILS †
Difficulty: 2

Assume that one day you're standing around with a friend waiting for a plane or train to arrive. You're both a little bored, so you pull out a quarter and start to flip it while your acquaintance "calls it" in the air. Soon the two of you are betting on several series of coin tosses. You hope that your series of three tosses occurs before your companion's series does, because then you win some agreed-upon amount. Look at these three bets:

You win when:	*Your acquaintance needs:*
A. 3 heads in a row come before	2 heads then 1 tail
B. 2 tails than 1 head come before	3 heads in a row
C. 2 heads then 1 tail come before	2 tails then 1 head

Are these fair bets? Work them out.

† Our thanks go to Professor David Pollard for this problem.

You've probably been told many times that there's an even chance of getting a head or tail on any one coin flip, regardless of what has come up on previous tosses. This is true,‡ but it doesn't necessarily follow that one series of coin tosses will occur as frequently as another series.

Look at the first bet shown above. You're betting that three heads in a row will come up before two heads and a tail. This is a fair bet. Two initial tails help neither player, but two initial heads help both. On the final toss, a head will make you win and a tail will give your acquaintance a victory. Since there is an equal chance of getting either a head or a tail on this last flip, neither player has an advantage. Really, you might have just bet on one coin (head or tail) but the series prolongs the game, adds tension, and sets your friend up for the kill!

The second bet, two tails then one head versus three heads, is more difficult to analyze. It appears to be fair at first glance, but in fact it is not a fair bet at all! Until the first two requirements of either series are completed, the game is even. After you have two tails or your companion has two heads, the advantage shifts to your side of the bet. It is possible for the player who is in the lead with two tosses to win on the third toss by getting the flip he needs to complete his series. Discounting this immediate possibility (which isn't, after all, very intriguing), something very interesting happens on the third toss. If your opponent has two heads and now a tail comes up, you have a start on completing your series. If you have two tails and then flip a third tail, you don't give your acquaintance any help at all, you simply keep yourself in the running. Three tails in a row means that you still have *two* tails in a row and can still win on the next toss. In fact, if you look closely at the problem, you should see that while your opponent can have two heads in a row and then still lose to you, once you get two tails in a row you can only win. A third tail will still give you two tails and a chance to win on the next toss, while a head gives you an immediate victory. In reality, you are flipping for a series of two while your companion and ex-friend is waiting for a series of three.

‡ A qualification: If the head side has a heavier engraved image (such as Lincoln's head), it will tend to go down (and the tail up) slightly more than half the time.

This advantage, of course, gives you a much better chance of winning. This result amazes most people and it should be clear in your mind before you bet your whole fortune. (While the odds are 3 to 2 in your favor, your opponent *could* win—so be safe and play for the first to attain ten victories. The averages will then have a chance to work in your favor.)

Now that you understand the intricacies of the second bet, you should see what is interesting about the third. Both sides of this wager resemble your series in the second bet, so that whichever player gets the first two flips of his series completed must necessarily win the bet. Essentially, the bet is two heads against two tails.

This problem, like the Sultan's Law, depends on an asymmetry that is designed to appear as a symmetry. Flipping coins is symmetrical, but series of coin flips are not necessarily symmetrical. You are safest betting on a clearly symmetrical series like three heads versus three tails or one-head-two-tails versus one-tail-two-heads unless, of course, you mean to take advantage of your new knowledge and garner some extra change.

Here's another problem with real life applications, but it's on a much grander scale than flipping coins. In truth, it is an economics example more than a puzzle, but it incorporates the idea of symmetry with some good solid reasoning and has never yet failed to entertain and engage.

SPATIAL COMPETITION I
Difficulty: 3

First, a relatively easy version of the problem serves as an introduction to the concepts involved. Once you have mastered these introductory concepts you will enjoy testing and entertaining friends using restaurant saltshakers and glasses for the shoe stores described below!

Imagine a society in which all businesses and residences are evenly distributed down one side of one long street. (Picture it as U.S. 1 running from Maine to Florida, with the other side of the street being beaches and water.) The shoe industry in this society is completely "undifferentiated"; all shoes are made by the same company, and all shoe stores are required to be exactly like all other shoe stores in terms of hours, prices, decor, sales help, and all other features except that of location. Therefore, there is no store or brand loyalty and all shoppers decide which store to patronize only on the basis of how close it is to where they live. Beyond that, they are equally indifferent to all the stores. (If you are not accustomed to the unrealistic models of economics, you might go back and read through all these assumptions one more time!)

1. Mr. A is planning to open the first shoe store and believes he will be the only one in the business. Where will he place his store to get the most business?

2. Mr. B sees Mr. A's success and decides to open his own shoe store but expects no further entry of shoe stores. Where will he open it? What about Mr. C, who is the third man to open his store (and also expects no further competition)?

3. What would happen if A, B, and C got together, before opening, and made an agreement on where to place their stores?

4. Is there any resolution to this situation? Think about it before reading the discussion that follows.

This is not an easy problem, but you should see that since Mr. A is the first to open his shoe business, he can place his store anywhere and still get all the shoe business of the society. Most likely, he will want customers to buy shoes instead of other things and, therefore, he'll open his store right in the middle of the length of the road, to make it most convenient for his customers.*

Florida   **A**   **Maine**
_____●_____

Think carefully now—where will Mr. B open his new shop? Then what about C?

Mr. B, being a shrewd businessman, looks at A's placement and decides to open his store right next to A. Because his store is now closer to half the population than A's is, he successfully steals half of A's business. Please convince yourself that spot x below is inferior because it loses half the customers between A and x.†

Florida   **X**   **BA**   **Maine**
_____●_____●●_____

* For the mathematically inclined reader, "convenience" here draws on a "least squares" or related notion. A long trip is weighted more heavily than two short trips, though the two short ones add up exactly to the one long trip.

The economically inclined reader might wonder whether rents vary along this road and whether the high rent in the middle does not exactly offset the increased business. Rather than going on to this subject for an entire chapter, we assume that rents and other costs are unrelated to store location.

† Of course, A and B could just as well divide up the customers by settling in anywhere on the line so long as they are equidistant from the center. If A were in Florida and B in Maine, they would be just as well off as when they are side by side in the center. On the other hand, if A were in Florida, B might be tempted to sneak from Maine in A's direction and then B would control more than one-half of the total. When the two competitors are at each other's sides in the center, there is, at least, no incentive to move a bit and hope to remain undetected. This tendency toward the center can be used to explain the similarity among the positions of political candidates on the eve of an election—each has moved toward the other in the hope of keeping the old faithful and attracting

When C is ready to open his store, he sees B's wise move and decides to put his store right next to A on the other side—thereby stealing the other half of A's business.

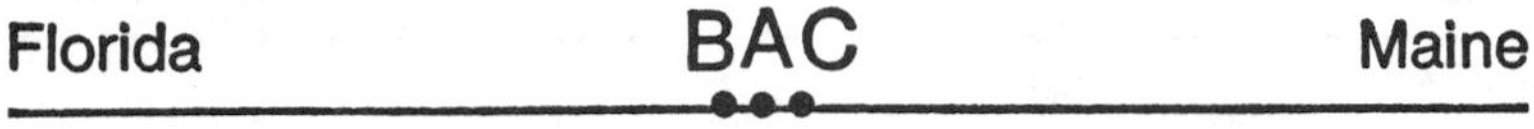

Mr. A must now move his store or go out of business. He hops over either B or C in order to regain *almost* half of his business. After this, the next store left in the middle must move, and then the next, continuing in a very unstable manner.

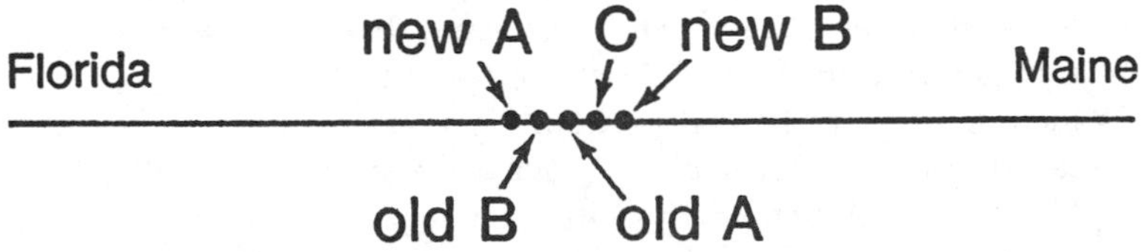

Will this continue until one is in Florida and another in Maine? No, because after a number of moves it will be more profitable to come back toward the center and draw customers from both directions.

If the three businessmen wanted to avoid all this jumping, they could try to talk everything over before opening any of the stores (although in the real world this is called collusion and is against the law) so that each got a fair share of the total business and saved all the moving expenses. This would probably lead to a situation in which the stores were placed at the $\frac{1}{6}$, $\frac{3}{6}$ ($\frac{1}{2}$), and $\frac{5}{6}$ positions along the road. So A gets the $\frac{1}{6}$ between his store and Florida and half of the $\frac{2}{6}$ (of the total) between himself and B, thus acquiring $\frac{1}{3}$ of the total business for himself. Similar calculations

---

the voters who are undecided. Similarly, various features of automobiles are remarkable similar across manufacturers.

show that we have what might be an "equilibrium" because each business has ⅓ of the total and would regard the deal as "fair."

Florida A	B	C Maine
1/6	1/2	5/6

Unfortunately, if one of the shoe store owners were tempted to "steal" a little more business from one of his competitors, he could start moving his store one way or the other and hope that his move would go undetected. Pretty soon the stores would start hopping around just as if they hadn't agreed on placement in the beginning. Can you think of a way that B can solve this problem if A is already positioned in the middle of the line and C has yet to arrive? Is there somewhere he can position his store so that everyone will be saved the cost and trouble of moving the stores continually?

The only resolution to this situation *might* come when a little more real-life is added to the problem. It's very expensive for stores to relocate even once, let alone over and over again, so chances are that once the stores had arranged themselves in a fairly equitable distribution they would stop moving because the further expenses would outweigh the potential benefits.

Alternatively, they might each give a sizable sum of money to a disinterested referee who would, for example, award the pot to A if B moved and to B if A were the violator. In the real world, once again, such a clever and farsighted arrangement is difficult to enforce (as it should be) because of the illegality of the whole thing. After all, while A and B are meeting to agree on locations they will be tempted to agree on raising prices together or act in concert to keep out future competitors.

Now for the tougher version:

SPATIAL COMPETITION II
Difficulty: 5

Think of the same problem, but this time the businesses and residences are on a *circular* highway with wasteland everywhere else. Four shoe stores are expected to open in this order: A, B, C, and D, and each knows about the other three. Where does the *second* store, Mr. B, open to get the most business? In this problem we will assume that *relocation is not possible* because the costs of moving are prohibitive. Once a store has opened, it is there to stay.

Work on this.

If you have thought about this problem for some time you should see that the whole question of store placement hinges on the *second* store, so asking about B is not just an arbitrarily selected question. Mr. A can open anywhere on the circle, but he cannot affect the arrangement of the stores that come after his grand opening. C (and then D) will put his store exactly in the middle of the largest space that remains when it is his turn to open.

For an example of how these principles will guide the four businesses, consider this run-through of the problem: A decides where he will open (on an empty circle it doesn't matter which location he chooses) and puts his business there. This, of course, is our old friend called symmetry. B decides to open his store directly across from A, so that the two are sharing all the business. If B tries to be cute and open next to A, for example, C might come just on his other side and leave B with no customers at all.‡

When it is C's turn to open, he looks at the circle and realizes that both open segments on the circle are of equal size. He can place himself in the middle of either side and capture a quarter of the business.

D's turn now comes last and he has three options. The open arcs are AC, CB, and AB, but D knows that going into AC or CB will give him a very small share of the business, so he decides to open in the middle of AB. See the illustration below. Each store ends up with a quarter of the total business.

‡ A very careful reader might argue that C will just as often go to *A's* other side and then B will end up with a huge clientele—assuming D does not squeeze out B. Perhaps we should have said that these owners prefer less risk and would not choose a strategy that meant large profits half the time but bankruptcy the other half. Opening *across* from A has the same "expected value" to B as many other choices and is also the safest move in many ways.

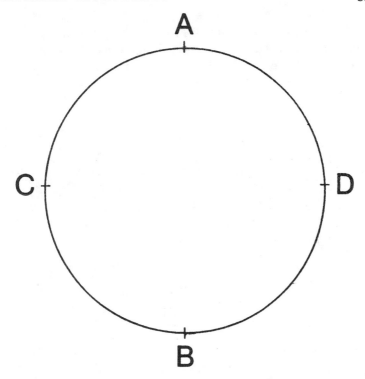

Only Mr. B can really control the arrangement of stores, so he ought to be able to place his store such that he gets more than one quarter of all the business. (Hint: Drawing circular diagrams can be a big help.) As was true in the simpler straight-line version of this problem, a symmetrical solution will give each store an equal business share—but this isn't what B has in mind. We have seen that each store gets a portion of the total business equal to the fraction of the circle he controls (half of the space on either side of him.) B wants to make sure that even after C and D open up, he will control *more* than a quarter of the circle.

Once you've got these aspects of the problem under control, it isn't too hard to find B's very best position through trial and error and a little arithmetic. B knows what will happen if he goes at the "½" mark directly across from A so he decides to experiment and think through the results of his going at the "⅓" mark to see if that's any better. B discovers that C will then go at the "⅔" mark, hoping that he can get half of all the business between A and B, and then B is left facing a two-to-one chance that D will choose to go on either side of him and greatly reduce his (B's) business.

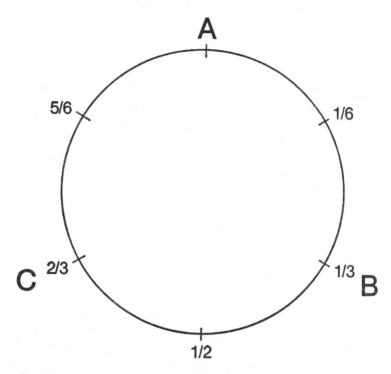

In other words, once A picks a spot and B goes to the "⅓" point and C to the "⅔" mark, D is indifferent among the "⅙," "½," and "⅚" locations. Sometimes (one third of the time) D will choose the "⅚" point and B will then have no competition from D. B will end up with one-half the business between himself and A ($\frac{1}{2} \times \frac{1}{3} = \frac{1}{6}$) plus the same ⅙ between himself and C. Thus, one third of the time B will be lucky and get one third of the total available business.

On the other hand, D is just as likely to choose the "⅙" or "½" locations and be adjacent to B. On B's other side B will enjoy ½ × ⅓ = ⅙, but on the side that now houses D only ⅙ of the circle is between B and D and B will get $\frac{1}{2} \times \frac{1}{6} = \frac{1}{12}$, which represents the group of people on that side closest to B's store. Thus, two-thirds of the time B will be patronized by $\frac{1}{6} + \frac{1}{12} = \frac{1}{4}$ of the total population.

In sum, B can expect, on average, $\frac{5}{18}$* of the total, which is *more* than the $\frac{1}{4}$ he enjoyed when opening at the "$\frac{1}{4}$" mark. (.277 is greater than .25.)

Now that you have seen that B can really do better than a $\frac{1}{4}$ share you are ready to look for the insight that will give him *even more* than this $\frac{5}{18}$ share. Try to experiment on your own.

---

* $(\frac{1}{4} + \frac{1}{4} + \frac{1}{3}) \div 3 = \frac{5}{6} \div \frac{3}{1} = \frac{5}{18}$

After a couple more tries, B (and you) will find the real trick to the problem. He abandons symmetry and begins to try positions that are just slightly to either side of one of the major divisions of the circle. The best solution B can discover is to position his store *slightly* closer to A than the ⅓ mark. C then splits the difference on the long arc between A and B and places slightly below the ⅔ mark.

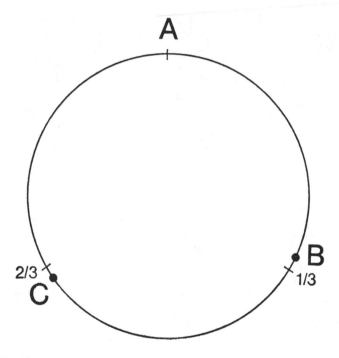

The distance AB is smaller than AC or CB, so D will not choose to open there. AC = CB, so there is now a 50 percent chance that D will place himself between C and B, cutting off some of B's business. If D goes on the far side of the circle from B, B will get approximately ⅓ of all the business, which is certainly better than his original ¼ share. If D decides to go between C and B, then B is left with approximately ¼ of the business. The average of these two possibilities for B is ⁷⁄₂₄ of the business—better than ¼ and better than ⁵⁄₁₈: B's great insight is to do something that will cause

D, most often, to choose a remote location that does not pull customers from B's pool of buyers.

There is a chance that A will come out with more customers than B some of the time, depending on where D places his store, but it's nothing that A or B can control (excluding the possibility of bribes), and B still does better than one-fourth of the business, on average. The clever principle here is that after B figures out his basic strategy he sees that his actual result depends on later actions (by C and D). B then acts—moving just a bit to the side—to encourage an otherwise indifferent D to take a course of action that helps B.

If we wanted to be very sophisticated we could allow bribes. A or C might pay D to open adjacent to B. The problem, in this light, gets very complex. You might write to us about this one!

S'MORE

Now is your chance to prove that you have understood and can use some of the problem-solving concepts we've introduced in this chapter. This next set of problems is presented without any revealing introductions or hints, but an explanation of each answer and how you might have come up with it follows each puzzle. Stop and do some work before reading the answers; you won't get any better at solving puzzles unless you try.

THE HUNDRED ARTISANS
Difficulty: 3

There was once a medieval Bavarian king named Gustav who loved to give lots of gold toys to the children of his kingdom every Christmas. To this end, he employed 100 skilled artisans to do nothing but make gold toys year-round. Every day, each artisan was given 16 ounces of gold to make a 1-pound toy.

A rumor suddenly reached Gustav one November that one of his artisans had been cheating him by using only 15 ounces of gold in his toys and keeping 1 ounce of gold a day for himself. The king was furious and decided that if the rumor were true and he could discover which of his artisans had been dishonest, that man would be executed immediately.

In the castle there was a very large graduated scale (like a doctor's office scale) which (miraculously, for Bavaria) registered in pounds and ounces. How could Gustav discover whether the rumor was correct and which artisan was guilty, by using the scale only once?

If you sorted through the tools at your disposal, you'll recognize this as a problem ripe for contraction analysis. The problem here is not that the artisans work with so much gold, because King Gustav's scale can handle all that weight. The real stumbling block is the number of artisans—one hundred just seems like too many to handle. Therefore, you begin contracting.

What would you do if there were just one artisan? You would weigh one of his toys and if it weighed 15 ounces you'd have your proof. What about two artisans? Your first impulse might be to weigh one toy from one artisan, figuring that if it weighed 15 ounces you had your man and if it weighed 16 then the other artisan must be guilty. This isn't exactly fair, though, considering that Gustav isn't even sure the rumor is true. This is the crux of the problem, and once you've solved it for two artisans, you've solved it for any number. Think again.

The trick is to take one toy from the first artisan and two toys from the second, and weigh all three together. If the toys come up 1 ounce short (47 ounces), the first artisan is guilty. If 2 ounces are missing then the second artisan is cheating, and if it weighs the correct amount (48 ounces), then both are honest men.

It should be easy to see how this contracted solution can now be expanded to fit the hundred artisans. The first supplies one toy, the second gives two, the third three, and so on up to the one hundredth artisan, who produces one hundred toys. If the toys weigh exactly what they should (5,050 pounds), then all the artisans are safe.† If there are any ounces missing, however, the number of missing ounces will indicate which artisan is cheating, and he will not be long for the world.‡ Pretty nifty solution.

---

† Do you know the trick for adding the numbers from 1 to 100? Look at it this way: $1 + 100 = 101$, and $2 + 99 = 101$. There are 50 such pairs of numbers, so $50 \times 101 = 5,050$.

‡ If the third artisan is cheating, for example, the toys will weigh only 5,049 pounds and 13 ounces—3 ounces short.

CAMELS
Difficulty: 3

An old Bedouin is lying on his deathbed and realizes he has only a few minutes left. He calls his three sons around him and tells them that he has very little to leave them, but that his first son shall inherit one half of all his property, his second son one third, and his third son is to get one ninth. Then the old man dies.

The three sons discover that their father left only seventeen camels and that the deathbed was rented. None of them wants to sell any camels, because the animals are worth more to these sons than anyone else would pay for them, but the sons can't figure out how to divide the camels according to their father's wishes. A wise camel-driver soon happens upon the three sons and hears their dilemma. In an instant, he has a somewhat inexact solution to their problem.

What is it?

This is a somewhat silly but cute problem that needs expansion, quite literally, to solve it. There are a couple of little tricks you've got to pick up on while you're working on it in order to find the solution. The first is to reduce the sons' fractions to a common denominator and then realize that the fractions don't add up to one. ($\frac{1}{2} + \frac{1}{3} + \frac{1}{9} = \frac{9}{18} + \frac{6}{18} + \frac{2}{18} = \frac{17}{18}$.) Second, you must notice that the common denominator (eighteenths) is more than coincidentally close to the number of camels.

The answer? Well, the wise man adds a camel of his own to the sons' herd, gives 9 to the first son, 6 to the second son, 2 to the third son, and then takes his own camel back. Each son gets a fraction of a camel more than he's supposed to, because their fractions, don't cover 100 percent of the property. This reasonably correct answer at least preserves the right ratios between the sons—the father might have meant for the second to get 3 times as much as the third ($\frac{1}{9} \times 3 = \frac{1}{3}$) and, sure enough, he gets 6 camels while the youngest gets 2 camels.

This puzzle should remind you again to keep your mind open to solutions that are out of the ordinary. They are often the most clever and satisfying (and perhaps *only*) answers.

TWELVE BALLS
Difficulty: 5

You are faced with twelve balls and a balance scale (which, un-like a graduated scale, tells you only whether the right pan's or left pan's contents are heavier). All but one of the balls are identical in weight; this oddball is either heavier or lighter than all the rest. You are allowed three weighings to discover which is the oddball and whether it's heavier or lighter. How do you do it?

Chances are you've seen this puzzle at least once and perhaps many times. If you can't remember or have never heard the answer, work on it for a little—or long—while. Solving this problem gives an enormous amount of satisfaction, because it's tough. If you already know the answer, you should still enjoy the following discussion. There are many interesting aspects to this problem that you might not have considered even if you have already discovered the solution.

The place to start, of course, is with the first weighing. A beginner might be tempted to start by weighing three against three. However, if this balances you're left with six unknown balls and two weighings and that, as some attempts will demonstrate, is a hopeless task. Starting with six balls against six balls does not give you enough useful information. One side of the scale will go down, the other up, and you still won't know where the oddball is. Five against five seems to look good, but if the first weighing does not balance you've got to do ten balls in two weighings, which is surely too many. If the first weighing *does* balance, you've got two weighings in which to do only two balls. This is easy and should indicate that you have too much work to do if this first weighing does *not* balance.

So by process of elimination we've settled that we start with four balls against four. (Admittedly, it's only really clear why you must start with four against four *after* you've solved the problem and have realized what your capabilities are with a balance scale.) There's a trick to the second weighing that is only discovered if you allow your mind to transcend the barriers that you've already set up in the problem. The three groups of four cannot remain inviolable. They must be mixed in most cases to make the second weighing useful.

Let's look at the case in which the first weighing balances. The oddball must be one of the remaining four. Only by weighing the uncertain balls against those that you know are "normal" can you find the one you're looking for, and by weighing three against three in the second weighing, you'll be left with one against one in the third weighing in order to get a definite answer. Therefore, you weigh three uncertains against three normals. If they balance, you'll know it's the fourth uncertain ball that's no good, and you need only weigh it against a good one to determine whether it's heavier or lighter. If the three against three do not balance, you will have found out that the oddball is one of the three uncertains on the scale, and you'll know whether it's heavier or lighter than the good balls. Now you need only weigh one of the three unknowns against another of these three. If they balance, then the third ball, which you left off the scale, is the culprit. If they don't balance, you also have your answer. If you already know the bad ball is light, then the ball on the high side is it. If you know the bad ball is heavy, then take the one on the low side.

Now let's return and consider the possibility that the first weighing did not balance. This gives you eight uncertain balls (four "heavy" and four "light"), and four (off the scale) that you know are good. There are many combinations of three on three that will work for your second weighing in this case, but it's most important to mix up heavies, lights, and normals on the scale (always keeping them straight in your mind). Weighing heavies against lights again might not yield new information.

The second weighing could be two heavies and one light on the left against two heavies and one light on the right. If it balances, then the oddball must be one of the two remaining lights. Just weigh one against a good one and you'll have your answer.

On the other hand, let's say they do not balance but that the right side goes down. The bad ball must be either the light on the left side or one of the heavies on the right. On your third weighing, weigh one of the heavies from the right pan against the other. If one side goes down, that's the one you want. Otherwise it must be the light one from the left pan. Are you still with us? You might use checkers or other objects in working this one through.

Let's try a different combination for the second weighing (still assuming that the first weighing did not balance). Place two heavies and one light on the left pan of the scale and one heavy, one light, and one good on the right side. If it balances, then the bad ball must be one of the three that you put aside: one heavy and two lights. Weigh one light against the other. If one side goes up then it's that one, otherwise the heavy is the oddball.

Now let's assume that the second weighing doesn't balance. If the right side again goes down, then the culprit is either the heavy on the right or the light on the left. Weigh either one against a good one to find out. If the left side goes down on the second weighing, then it's one of the two heavies on the left or the light on the right, and you already know how to deal with that situation.

There are more possible combinations, but by now you should be able to figure out what to do in any situation. If all of this has just been a review for you, then you should start thinking about how you could change the puzzle to make it more challenging for you. Learning how to create new puzzles should also make it easier for you to solve existing puzzles. In our "Loose Ends" section at the end of the chapter we'll deal with some of the variations on the twelve-ball problem. How about *two* oddballs, or an imaginary balance scale with three pans? Would it be easier or harder if you compared the balls by their water displacement rather than their weight? How many balls do you think you could do with four instead of three weighings? (This one might surprise you.)

The final problem in the chapter is the toughest and longest of all, but fascinating in its possibilities and real life applications. You're going to need all your wits to deal with this challenge, so gather them and proceed cautiously.

DIVISION OF LAND
Difficulty: 86

A dying father wants to leave his land to his three (or four) daughters. It is very important to him that they not fight in the future, so he is looking for a method of division that will leave no daughter feeling that any other daughter's share is better than her own. Do not suggest that he sell the land and divide the money in three or four (giving any spare pennies to charity) because the land has great sentimental value and each square inch of land is worth more to the family members than any acre is to an outsider.

Work on this for a good long time and then read on.

This is an example that might have convinced you to follow the earlier advice in this chapter and simplify by contraction—with unfortunate results. The same problem with *two* daughters was discussed in the introduction to this book and is the familiar situation in which friends or siblings cut a dessert in half. Here "you cut, I choose" has become so familiar a solution that we tend to overlook its elegance. If B is the cutter, A gets to choose between the two pieces. B, who presumably cut the pie, the land, or the child so that she was indifferent between the two halves, cannot now complain that A's portion is more attractive.

How about three daughters and three portions? With the dessert example in mind, you might imagine that B could begin to cut the dessert and as she moves the knife over the pie she tells A and C that they should yell "stop" when B's knife is about to cut a piece big enough so that A (or C) will feel she is getting at least one third of the pie. B then begins to move the knife over an increasing part of the pie. Once B moves to a point at which she thinks one third has been reached, she could mark the pie there and tell A and C to play "you cut, I choose" with the rest. This solution appears to be convenient (and uses contraction to boot), but the job is not really done.

Recall the requirements of the problem: Once the dividing is over, no party should feel that someone else received a better piece. In this solution, while B may feel that she got one third or even more of the pie, when she sees the way in which C now divides the remainder in half she might want to come back (reenter) and say, "If I had known that you would divide the remainder in this way, I would have preferred that piece over there which is much better than my one-third." This is a very interesting problem with many side issues and applications to real-world issues, so you might want to stop here and rethink the problem.

Note another, more clever but also unfortunate, contraction approach. Following the "you cut, I choose" model, A is asked to divide the pie into three parts so that she would be happy with any of the three (with B and C getting the other two). B and C then indicate their preferences. Of course if they choose different portions (as divided by A) then we are home free and give A the remaining part. Since this is a hard problem, we can assume that B and C prefer the same piece—call it piece 1 of the three pieces. Now ask them to make a second choice. If B and C still agree and point to piece 2, then give piece 3 to A and let B and C play "you cut, I choose" with the sum of 1 and 2. Similarly (but with a bit more complication), if B's second choice is 2 and C's is 3 let them play "you cut . . ." with piece 1 and let each play "you cut . . ." with A for the second-choice pieces. Thus, A gets "half" of 2 and "half" of 3. This appears to be confusing enough to be right! It uses contraction and cleverly lets A be even better off in many cases.

Unfortunately this solution also suffers from the "reenter" problem. This is best seen in the case in which B and C have identical first and second choices. They play "you cut . . ." with 1 and 2 according to the suggested solution. However, at this point A might reenter and say, "If I had known you would redivide 1 and 2 in this manner I would have told you that I prefer one of these new portions to 1, 2, or 3 alone." In this way the solution fails because A may well be honestly dissatisfied.

Let's return to the original division of land example to illustrate this problem of reentry. A, in the figure below, has already divided the land into three parts 1, 2, and 3, but B and C both like 1 as a first choice and 2 as a second choice. B divides 1 and 2 with the dashed line. But now A can claim that the outlined triangle (xyz) is much better than plot 3. It might contain beautiful trees (denoted by circles in the diagram), whereas A's initial division clearly assigned one tree to each parcel. Perhaps B and C never even noticed or cared about the trees.

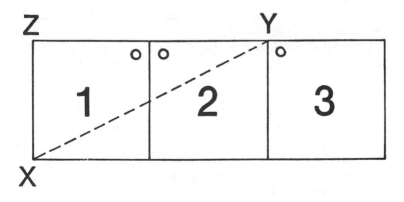

There are a number of ways to proceed at this point. With patience and imagination you might have developed a satisfactory approach on your own. For example, you might have tried a bidding scheme. The land could be divided into many very small pieces (say 1,000) and each daughter could be given 1,000 chips (for example) with which to bid for the pieces of land. This seems like a good solution, because the daughters get to allot their chips to the pieces of land that are the most valuable to them.

The one strong objection to this solution is that one daughter might end up dissatisfied if her two sisters collude. B and C, for example, could alternate outbidding A on her favorite choices, and A would end up feeling that the others had come out better.

To overcome this objection, the authority who is charged with carrying out the father's wishes might say, when the bidding was finished, that this had been a trial run and the real bidding would take place the following day. This would give A a chance to bribe B or C if she saw they were going to collude against her. Somehow, this whole situation is messy. (If you're a practical sort and worry that dividing the land into small pieces will result in no one's getting a contiguous set of plots, read on to our explanation of rents.)

For our purposes, the problem is better solved by a method that is cute (always a plus) and useful for the more complicated problem in which there are *four* daughters who must each get a piece of land.

The key element in solving this problem is to note from our previous failures that a strategy is defeated when a new party who is not the original divider comes in to make new divisions. It is always after a second divider steps up that we hear the complaint that the daughter who had once been happy is no longer so pleased. With this in mind the key is always to rely on the first divider to do all the splitting according to her own tastes. This way she can never come back to haunt us with her complaints.

How can you do this? Let A divide the land into three parcels that are equal in her view. Again B and C both prefer parcel 1. Do you see what to do? Let *A* make piece 1 less attractive (trying to discourage B and C from sticking to the same piece) by taking bits away from 1 and dividing the bits into 2 and 3 (making them bigger) so that A is still happy getting either 2 or 3. Do you see the

idea? We don't commit A to a single plot in this solution and we
remain with just one divider. Eventually either B or C will say, "I
like the new and enlarged parcel 2 (or 3) better than the shrinking
parcel 1, and I'll move to that one." A then gets parcel 3 (or 2)
and the remaining daughter who did not budge gets her first choice
—the somewhat smaller piece 1. An elegant solution.

It seems that there are two objections to this solution. First, it is
unrealistic to have A take off a little bit from the prize parcel in
each step. Let's call this task *shaving*—in this case shaving from 1
into 2 and 3. Perhaps this objection is best answered by imagining
that the problem concerns a huge amount of land with buildings
of every sort. The daughters are dividing up such an estate and
have different preferences based on their opinions as to the future
rents they can earn from owning various bits of land and buildings.
Shaving might involve taking $\frac{1}{50}$ of the future rents from a sky-
scraper in package 1 and putting $\frac{1}{100}$ into each 2 and 3. This example is particularly appealing because it resembles the actual pro-
cedures used in dissolving partnerships. Occasionally one comes
across such parceling and "you cut, I choose" bargaining in local
newspaper descriptions of real-estate partnership dissolutions.

A second objection to the shaving solution is that B and C may
have *exactly* the same tastes and the solution will fail. Perhaps at
the very moment that A has shaved sufficiently for B to move into
2, C also indicates that she now prefers parcel 2. Of course, A
might try a smaller shaving, but B and C might again move from 1
to 2 at the same instant. This objection is really no objection at all,
but rather an indication of the solution's success. At worst we have
the problem of getting so close to discovering the tastes of the par-
ties that plots 1 and 2 (post-shaving) may be equally acceptable to
daughters B and C. The more B and C move back and forth together (prolonging the settlement process and irritating A, no
doubt) the more they demonstrate to us the identity of their tastes.
And if, in effect, B and C have identical tastes, then we can satisfy
the requirements of the problem by giving parcel 1 to one sister and
parcel 2 to the other. A, of course, is amply pleased with the now
expanded parcel 3 and no daughter feels that one of her sisters got
a better parcel than she. Thus, the response to the second objection
is that while no one may feel that her parcel is the *uniquely* best

parcel, it doesn't matter, because this was never the goal of the exercise. We were only asked to be sure that no one would prefer the inheritance of another.

Once this solution is accepted, we have moved a long way toward solving the same problem for four daughters—a problem thought insoluble by many authors.

The four daughters are A, B, C, and D. Have A divide the land into four plots such that she would be happy with any of them. Call the plots 1, 2, 3, and 4. The other three daughters indicate their preferences. Needless to say we are stuck with somewhat similar tastes for the purpose of the problem. Perhaps B and C settle into plot 1 and D chooses 2. Now A must shave from 1 into 2, 3, and 4. (We might have had the shaving done into 3 and 4, figuring that we can leave well enough alone in plot 2. However, as we increase 3 and 4 we can count on D's increasing jealousy and her re-entry, so we take this into account at the outset.) A continues the shaving until B or C moves into a new plot. Whenever two daughters are in the same plot (or three in the same plot), as when B moves into 2 in competition with D, A turns her attention to that plot and shaves from it into all the others (from 2 into 1, 3, and 4).

This solution is much better than it first seems. It only fails in the sense of the second objection to the solution for three daughters, as above. A may need to shave tiny pieces here and there—but this is part of the game and is a sign of the solution's success, not failure. When A is stooping to infinitely small shavings, we will know our task is done.

As you can see, this division problem is about as difficult as any problem you will ever encounter. The problem and the solution are attractive on many counts. We have long been familiar with the procedure for solving the problem with two people. Children can often be seen splitting desserts with this widely accepted method. The problem is a good illustration of how common solutions can be expanded to work in challenging problems. The solution for three daughters is interesting because it shows that a simple expansion of the two-person solution does little good. The condition of happiness is violated. Shaving proves to be a useful and novel idea. While it is silly for dividing cake (shaved crumbs are no fun) it does make sense for some very real problems, such as dividing up partnerships. The most interesting aspect of shaving is that it does the trick for three *and* four people. In fact, it looks useful for *any* number of claimants, subject to the "objection" that we might need infinitely small shavings until we can declare with confidence that people are equally happy (indifferent, in economics) with any of two or more packages.

A final note: While our statement of the problem disallowed selling the land and simply dividing the money among the three or four daughters, it might be argued that in any "real world" problem, a sale is the practical solution. But this is not quite so. Land might have sentimental value. Partnership holdings may require expert management and apart from the few people who are trying to divide the property there may be no comparable experts and, therefore, no one who will pay enough to satisfy the property holders. In other words, one third the *market* value of the property may be far less than what would please any of the daughters. A sale may also force a payment of taxes and commissions, while dividing the land can avoid these charges. In fact, then, each daughter might prefer almost any division of the land over such a sale and distribution of proceeds.

LOOSE ENDS

This section is for tidbits that somehow didn't fit into the body of the chapter. Some of the bits are closely related to the problems in the chapter and others are not, but all should prove interesting.

Bridge Crossing. Do you remember the brave fellows who crossed the treacherous bridge at the beginning of the chapter? In case you still thought you could somehow get away with a solution different from ours, here's an analysis that shows why you can't.

THEOREM: The problem requires at least five moves.

PROOF: Each move must involve either one person or two according to the statement of the problem. If one person first crosses alone then he must return with the lantern, wasting time. Therefore, two people will cross on the first trip (1). If the two people return, we're back where we started, so only one person will return with the lantern (2). If one person crosses now, we're back to where we were after the first move, so two men cross (3). The only way for the last man to get across is for one man to return (4) and take him back (5).

Here's a separate argument:

THEOREM: If "20" and "25" move separately, it's impossible to use fewer than 65 minutes.

PROOF: If "20" and "25" cross separately, the two trips will add up to 45 minutes. As proved above, there must be at least three more trips. At least one of the trips will be made by "10" (to avoid making the slow men cross more than once), and even if the other two are made by "5," that requires 20 minutes more of crossing time. Total time: 65 minutes. Therefore, "20" and "25" must go together for the problem to be solved.

Variations on Weighing Twelve Balls. If you were very methodical while solving the twelve-ball problem, you might have come up with a chart like the one that follows. It first identifies all the balls with numbers and specifies their placement during each of the three weighings. The second half of the chart shows which ball is the oddball, and whether it is heavy or light, according to which side of the scale goes down in each of the three weighings. (L is left, R is right, E means the pans are even.)

Weighing:	Left side	Right side	Off
1	5, 6, 7, 8	9, 10, 11, 12	1, 2, 3, 4
2	2, 8, 11, 12	3, 4, 9, 10	1, 5, 6, 7
3	1, 4, 6, 10	3, 7, 9, 12	2, 5, 8, 11

Ball:	Heavy	Light
1	EEL	EER
2	ELE	ERE
3	ERR	ELL
4	ERL	ELR
5	LEE	REE
6	LEL	RER
7	LER	REL
8	LLE	RRE
9	RRR	LLL
10	RRL	LLR
11	RLE	LRE
12	RLR	LRL

The chart is very easy to use. For example, if the scale balances on the first weighing, the right side goes down on the second weighing, and the left side goes down on the third (ERL), then the fourth ball must be heavy.

If you're inventive, you can probably think of many ways to alter or expand the counterfeit ball problem. Here are a few extra twists that make the puzzle more challenging, especially if you've already mastered the problem as it was originally stated.

What would happen to the problem (and solution) if you used water displacement to compare the balls instead of weighing them on the balance scale? If you consider this change, you'll see that it is similar to using two graduated scales instead of a balance scale. The water displacement method would not only indicate which balls were heavier or lighter, it would give a precise quantitative measurement against which to compare balls. For example, if the first four against four weighing balances, you know not only that they are good balls, but also exactly how much four (and therefore one) good balls should displace. When you try to find the unknown ball from among the four remaining, the measurement of displacement will tell you if it's heavy or light even before you compare it to a good ball. This method might still require three weighings to find the counterfeit ball, but it makes it easier to gather more information from each weighing.

Another interesting variation uses a three-pan balance scale instead of a two-pan scale. Although it's hard to picture, it's clear that this scale would greatly simplify solving the problem. The first weighing (four against four against four) would tell you which group of four contained the counterfeit ball and whether it was heavier or lighter. (Two of the three pans would have to balance, and the third would be either heavier or lighter.) The problem is so easily solved in three weighings that you could deal with many more than twelve balls and still find the answer.

A much more difficult variation involves *two* counterfeit balls. We've worked on the version in which both oddballs are heavy or both are light (HH or LL). (If the two counterfeit balls are not necessarily the same weight [HL], the problem becomes extremely difficult, as you can see if you work on it at all. Simply put, even when two against two balances, we need more information because a heavy may be opposite a light on the scale. We could declare that a heavy is heavier than a light is light—and that the scale would tip—but this gets too complicated. Write to us if you're interested in these possibilities!)

Can you handle two oddballs (HH or LL) in a group of six in three weighings?

If you thought about the chart method of doing the twelve-ball problem, you saw that two oddballs *cannot* necessarily be isolated from six balls. Look at it this way. If the first weighing favors the left pan (L), then there are nine possible combinations of outcomes: LLL, LLE, LLR, LEL, LEE, LER, LRE, LRL, LRR. Similarly, if the first weighing balances (E), there are nine other configurations, as are there nine if the first weighing favors the right pan. Therefore, there are twenty-seven outcomes. The twelve-ball problem could be done because it required twenty-four possible configurations—each of the twelve balls could be heavy or light. But there are fifteen possible pairs in a group of six. These pairs are: 1-2 (balls 1 and 2), 1-3, 1-4, 1-5, 1-6, 2-3, 2-4, 2-5, 2-6, 3-4, 3-5, 3-6, 4-5, 4-6, and 5-6. If each pair can be HH or LL, then we'll need thirty configurations of weighing results—and we only have twenty-seven in the three shots that are allowed.

With this insight, you ought to wonder whether the twelve-ball problem could be extended to thirteen balls, since it looks like thirteen balls would require twenty-six configurations. Unfortunately, the answer is no, because, as you might see, weighing four balls against three is of little use. To derive maximum information from our weighings, we need a number of objects that is divisible by the number of weighings. We do best in these three-weighings problems by dealing with the balls in piles of three each.

Two oddballs (HH or LL) are easily isolated in a group of three balls. Begin with ball 1 against ball 2 and if, for example, the right side goes down, then ball 3 is either the light twin of 1 or the heavy twin of 2. Try 1 against 3 to see which it is.

Can the problem be done with a group of five balls? Four? Your time is probably better spent with pregnant women.

Pregnant Women. Here's one last example of contraction in action. The technique used should remind you of the way we solved the family size question in the Sultan's Law problem, and it's a technique that can easily be applied to other similar situations.

Can you estimate what percentage of all women of childbearing age (in the United States) are pregnant at any given time? Work on it awhile.

If you didn't catch the hint (pun) about contraction, you probably started by trying to figure how many women are in the country and how many of them are of childbearing age. You also probably didn't get too far this way. Contraction is the key.

Start thinking of the problem in terms of one average woman. Given our country's birthrate, she (over her lifetime) will have slightly more than 2 kids (on average, remember). This means about 18 months of pregnancy. Now add to those 18 months the amount of time some women are pregnant before having an abortion or miscarriage. Maybe 3 months? Or 6? Even 9 as a national average? That brings the (average) total months of pregnancy to between 21 and 27. Now you can estimate her prime childbearing years as running from about 17 years old to about 39—a time span of 22 years (264 months). This means she spends approximately 10 percent of her childbearing years pregnant, and the figure should apply to all women.

The elegance of this method is that even though it requires a series of estimations, the end result cannot be too far off the mark. One gets a rough estimate that is surprisingly accurate considering that only common knowledge was used.

Now for a little fun, try estimating the number of McDonald's in the United States or the number of miles of roads in the country. (Hint: The answer to one of these questions is about 5,000 and the answer to the other is almost 4 million.)

2

Small Games and Diversions

Now that you have gained a little expertise in solving problems, we're going to put you to some new challenges. Chapter 2 contains a few more puzzles and introduces some great games to play. Analyzing these games can be surprisingly similar to analyzing puzzles, but the differences are intriguing and will prepare you for the original games in chapter 3. In the event that you're getting too engrossed in puzzles, we've included some real-life applications of the kinds of analyses you are learning.

The first game we'd like to introduce is Indian Poker, a game that may already be familiar to you. Rules for the standard game and some variations follow. (It probably helps to be acquainted with regular forms of poker.)

INDIAN POKER

Equipment: A standard deck of playing cards.
Object: To win money!
Play: You can play with any size group from two to fifty-two people, but our rules are slightly different for fewer than six people. As in other poker games, all players ante (put in some money) before the hand begins. The dealer then deals one card face down to each player, including herself. At a signal from the dealer each player lifts her card up *with the face away from herself* and holds it to her own forehead. Thus, the players see each others' cards but never their own.

The players bet only once, starting at the dealer's left and proceeding around the table. When the betting is completed, each person, in order around the table, must declare whether she is going "high" or "low." The Ace of spades is "high" and the Two of clubs is "low." (With fewer than six people, the game is played only for high, so declaration is omitted.) Then all cards are removed from the players' foreheads, revealed to these owners, and the winners split the pot.

Discussion: It's easy to see what happens in this game. Everyone tries to guess, from looking at other players' cards and from the betting, what her own card must be. It's difficult to describe an optimal betting strategy, since the game is mostly luck and psychology. On the other hand, if you hold an Ace on your forehead, your opponents have a clue and will go "low," unless they try to trick you into thinking that you have a very low card showing. To make the game more open to analysis, the players need more information with which to plan their strategies. Remember that the player to the left of the dealer has the roughest time, so that in the interests of fairness the dealership should rotate.

The following variations of Indian Poker are easy to understand and more interesting to play. You'll have more of a chance to develop your puzzle theory, because skill becomes more important in winning.

INDIAN POKER TIMES EIGHT

In this variation, each player antes one chip unless the *average* of all the cards she sees is greater than eight—in which case she must ante two chips. This gives each player more information about her own card than in the standard game. The unknown element remains, but the game is no longer so luck-oriented.

INDIAN BLACKJACK

The dealer deals one card down, which the player can look at, and one forehead card to each player. To make the game even more interesting, one can bet before the second card is dealt. The game proceeds like regular blackjack, with additional cards and betting. A player wins the bet if her cards are closer to 21, when summed, than are the dealer's cards. More than 21 always loses.

This game reduces the importance of the hidden card even more, although it still plays a crucial role in winning. As the importance of the hidden card decreases, the possibilities for analysis and intelligent strategies by the players increase.

INDIAN CHOOSE

This game allows for the most control by strategic and analytic players. Those averse to risks can choose to ignore the forehead card altogether. As in Indian Blackjack, the dealer deals one card down and one card to the forehead. Betting and declaring of high and low proceed as in the original Indian Poker. When it comes to the final revelation, however, each player chooses whether she wants to include only her down card (which she alone has seen) or only her forehead card (which she alone has *not* seen). This can be a very tantalizing game, because a player doesn't know whether to bet against the odds of what might be turned down or against the cards she can see. Furthermore, it's hard to tell whether another player is betting heavily on the strength of her hole card or because she thinks she's figured out the identity of her forehead card.

Indian Poker and its variations introduce an important variable that can be used to modify games you already like: Who gets to see what? In some games there are elements that only you see, in others, elements that everyone sees, and in others, elements that everyone *but* you can see.

In the game of War, *no one* gets to see the elements. This game is totally dependent on luck. You're probably familiar with this simple game, but it's fun to play and serves as a good harbinger of the games that follow.

WAR

Equipment: A standard deck of playing cards.

Object: To wipe out your opponent's cards.

Play: The game is for two players, although it would be easy to expand the game to accommodate more. The dealer shuffles the deck and deals out the entire deck to herself and her opponent (see the later discussion for other ways to divide the deck).

Each player keeps her pile of cards face down in front of her. Both players simultaneously lift up their top card and place it face up in the middle of the table. Whoever has the higher card wins the round and adds both these cards to her separate "take" pile. Play continues until the original card piles are gone. Each player then shuffles her "take" pile and uses it to resume play. When one player has collected the whole deck, the game is over.

In the event of a tie between face-up cards, the players must have a "war." Suppose each player has put down an Eight. The original cards remain on the table, and each player places her next three cards face down next to her first card, then turns a fourth card up beside all of them. The fourth card decides the whole battle and the winner takes all ten cards. If the fourth cards tie as well, the process is repeated so that eighteen cards are on the table. (If one player runs out of cards, shorten the "war.")

Discussion: Since this game is based completely on luck and therefore is not susceptible to strategy, it tends to delight children and frustrate adults. It's possible to begin with equal endowments by dividing the deck into suits and giving each player two suits. However, shuffling the two piles makes the game random again. Luck determines the final outcome no matter how you divide the deck, but beginning with two entire suits per player makes the game last longer.

You only have to use one element of luck to add randomness to a game. For example, the process of deciding in what order players will take turns in any board game can proceed in several ways. Often the players will roll dice, and the highest number goes first, the next highest second, and on to the lowest roller, who goes last. However, it would work just as well if the players all rolled dice, decided that the highest roll would go first, and proceeded around the table. Both methods are equally random, since the highest roll is a matter of luck.

This might remind you, as it did us, of a problem with the military draft lottery a few years ago. The system was random; anyone born on the dates that were blindly chosen in the lottery was subject to the draft in the order his number was chosen. On this occasion, however, a number of the early dates that were chosen were in March. A lawsuit was brought against the Selective Service System claiming that the numbers must not have been mixed well enough because the drawing was not statistically random.

Our point is that this drawing was fair despite the large number of March dates. It would be just as fair to select in random fashion one day of the year and then proceed from that date, because the choice of the commencement point is still a matter of luck.

PLANNED WAR

As in the variations of Indian Poker, Planned War reduces the randomness of the original game and allows the players more control over their playing strategies.

Two, three, or four can play. Each player is given one complete suit from the deck of cards, which she may pick up and look at. Before each round, or trick, each player decides which card to throw into the center of the table—always hoping that her card will exceed those of her opponents. All players must put out their cards simultaneously. If a tie occurs in Planned War, it might be wise to take those cards back and replay the trick, since a "war" would use up a lot of cards. Clearly, the idea is to try to win a round by a small margin or lose by a large one. Thus, if you think your opponent will put out a King you would want to put out your Ace or your Deuce (if your Ace is gone).

FIXED WAR

This is played like Planned War, except that each player sets up the order in which her cards will be played before the rounds begin. Each pile is then placed face down on the table and the order of the cards cannot be changed during the game.

Discussion: It would seem that in these games a group of players would come out equal in wins and losses. After all, you're playing with the same cards and one suit does not overpower another. Surprisingly, this doesn't always happen. The more you play with a certain person, the more you learn about her habits and strategies, and with this information you should be able to win more than 50 percent of the time (unless of course she's working just as hard to figure *you* out).

THE PRICE IS RIGHT

You're probably more than familiar with the television game show "The Price Is Right." Doesn't it remind you of Planned War in some way? Instead of trying to be higher than all your opponents, you're trying to be closer to a specified price *without exceeding that price.*

If you're lucky enough to go last, the best strategy should be obvious. After you've decided on what you think is the correct price, you simply see which guess was closest to that figure but below it, and then guess one dollar more. One way to improve the game and reduce the advantage of going last would be for the producers to offer a $1,000 bonus if the closest bid turns out to be within $5.00 of the real price. The simple strategy would still work, but the incentive to guess closer to your estimated correct price would be much stronger. The best way to reduce the advantage of being the first or last to guess would be to have the bids given in simultaneously, without any player having knowledge of the guesses put forward by the other players.

Here's an example of the simple strategy: You and three other contestants must guess the price of a color TV, and you get to guess last. In your mind, you decide that the price of the set is close to $595 (or at least between $450 and $650). The first contestant guesses $600. The second contestant guesses $650 and the third guesses $350. The "right" guess for you to make is $351, even though something like $575 is closer to your estimate of the price. If you were playing a version with the $1,000 bonus, it might then be worthwhile to venture a guess that is closer to your real estimate, since, for most people, the $1,000 is worth the risk that is involved.

Doesn't this remind you of Spatial Competition? Here, the *third* player has the toughest choice because she must reason in reverse order and consider the action that the fourth player will take. It would be wise not to give the fourth player too much working room, so a $535 bid by the third player would have been better than the $350 bid.

Now we've seen games (like Planned War) in which you try to exceed your opponent's bids and one in which you try not to overshoot the target price. In the games that follow, you try to match your opponent and she tries *not* to match you.

TEN NUMBERS GAME

Play: This game is useful in entertaining a child from six to ten years old. It is for two players who sit across a table from each other. Each player has a blank sheet of paper, and a book or another small child is propped up between them so neither can see the other's paper. Each player writes a column of ten single-digit numbers (from o through 9) down the page. The players don't have to use every number; they can repeat some and leave others out of the list.

Player 1 chooses her ten numbers in the hope that she will match player 2's list as much as possible—the correct numbers in the right positions. Player 2 chooses her numbers to outwit player 1, hoping that nothing at all will match.

Since there are ten digits and ten spaces in the sequence, player 1 should average one match with player 2. Whether the players try to match on just one number (player 1 can write o through 9 and so can player 2) or on a list of numbers, 1 in 10 times there will be a match, on average. Plainly, if player 2 put down a 3, 1 in 10 times player 1 will be lucky and match it. So, if the two play ten times (ten digits), then, on average, they will match one time ($\frac{1}{10} \times 10 = 1$).

Thus, one match should be considered a draw. If there are no matching pairs, player 2 has been successful and wins. If more than one pair match, player 1 wins.

This game can easily include betting. If there are no matches, player 1 owes player 2 one dollar. If there is more than one match, player 2 owes player 1 a dollar for each match over one.* One match is still a draw. Betting increases the incentive for the players to outguess each other.

This is another game in which randomness should control the outcome, but psychology and knowledge of the way your opponent thinks can tip the game in your favor. Mixing up your numbers is

---

* Increasing the payoff for more than two matches makes this game less than "fair" to player 2, who is on the defense. Therefore, it is important to count the rounds carefully to be sure that each player is allowed the same number of turns in the offensive role (which player 1 is enjoying in this illustration).

the risk-averse strategy. Grandstand plays such as writing ten 3's or the numbers 0 through 9 in order can lead to big victories if you read your opponent's mind accurately, but these strategies can also cause large losses. You are best off sticking to the risk-averse strategy if you like to play it safe.

FINGER BASEBALL

Warning: This is one of the greatest and most habit-forming games to play.

Equipment: Just your hand.

Object: To score more runs in nine innings than your opponent.

Play: Two people play; each is one baseball team. Just as in regular baseball, the teams alternate batting and playing defense. Each team gets three outs; there are no balls, no strikes, and no fouls. Dugouts and popcorn are optional.

All of the action in this game depends on the finger configurations of the two players. In a motion similar to "shooting" for "odds or evens," the two players extend one to five fingers to mean certain things:

> one finger = a single
> two fingers = a double
> three fingers = a triple
> four fingers = a walk
> five fingers = a home run

(Some people play that four is a home run and five is a walk, so you should get this straight before you start. Of course, if you're losing you can always jump up and shout that you learned it the other way.) At first you may have to signal each other when you're ready to "shoot," but soon you'll fall into the rhythm of it. It's great during class.

Say that X is at bat and Y is in the field. If *both* players put up one finger, then X gets a single. If X puts up one finger and Y puts up anything else, then X has one out. In other words, if X and Y match, X receives whatever reward is indicated by the number of fingers, and if X and Y do not match, X is out. Runners on base advance as many bases as the batter when X gets a hit, but when the batter walks, they only move if forced by a player behind them.

Think you've got it? Play a few games.

Finger Baseball seems similar to Planned War and some of the other games in this section. You'd expect to match your opponent about 20 percent of the time (on-base percentage of .200), and split wins and losses pretty evenly. However, playing frequently should clue you in to playing strategies so that you can outguess most players. It is astonishing how little chance a beginner has against an expert.

The difference between this game and Planned War is that in Planned War you have a fixed set of options (your cards) which you can use only once. In Finger Baseball, you can use as many "aces" as you wish, but your opponent can foil you by not matching. What seems to be your best move may not work at all.

What should you shoot with runners on first and second and two outs? On first thought it seems like a walk (four fingers) might be a good idea, since your opponent will probably be shooting something that won't help you too much even if you *do* match. A walk won't bring a run in (your opponent thinks) but it will prolong the inning (you think). But look again. If your opponent thinks along similar lines she might predict a four from you and deliberately avoid it. A clever strategy for her might be to throw a triple or a home run, because it's what *you* want most of all but would never believe she'd give you.

As a reward for reading this book, here is a surprisingly successful way to beat a real greenhorn (whom you have just taught). In the first inning when you are at bat, begin with a five and then follow with a one on the second batter. Now come back with a five. Frequently your first five will have succeeded in planting a seed in your opponent's head and your new victim will only conceal her appetite for a daring defense play for one interim batter. You may even get a single out of the second batter.

Are you getting a sense of some of the neat twists to this game? It's great to teach people to play, because most people have been exposed to baseball all their lives and are familiar with some of the strategy. The game looks as if it's based on luck, but it proves to be more complicated and interesting. It's also a very easy game to handicap (with extra outs) and thereby accommodate the difference in expertise between players.

Here's a puzzle that really looks like a game because the solution depends so much on the other participants. It *is* a puzzle though, since you can't play it twice the same way.

COLORED HATS

Four women, who have been told that all those present are very intelligent, are sitting in a testing room. A tester enters the room and puts a hat on each woman's head, and then tells them that each is now wearing either a black or white hat. The tester asks each woman to stand up if she can see two black hats, and to raise her hand if she has determined the color of her own hat.

All four women immediately stand up, and after a few minutes one woman raises her hand. She correctly identifies the color of her hat. What was its color? How did she deduce it?

Work on this before reading on.

You're probably familiar with this puzzle for *three* people, but we included it anyway because it's such a perfect example of contraction. If you are familiar with the three-person version, you have an enormous head start. If not, you probably should have thought of contraction anyway.

The three-person variation is the same as the four-person puzzle, except that the three women are asked to stand up if they see *one* black hat. All three women stand up, and then one raises her hand and announces her color.

She says her hat must be black, because if it were white each of the other two women would see one white and one black. They would then know *they* were each black because otherwise the woman *they* saw with the black hat wouldn't have stood up. Got it?

The answer to the four-person problem rests on the three-person problem. The woman who raised her hand announced that she must have a black hat, because if she had a white hat the remaining three women would be reduced to the three-person problem, which they would have solved as above (or, better yet, heard at a cocktail party).

The five-person version of this problem is probably ridiculous because you can't count on people, other than geniuses and those with enough time to read a book like this one, to make the correct deductions. In a game with real people, this would probably be true, but in a puzzle we can state that all five women are very intelligent and all are aware that their companions are equally clever. We assume that they do, indeed, make all the correct deductions.

Again, a hat is placed on each woman's head and she is told it is either black or white. The women are told to stand up if they see two black hats, and to raise their hands if they guess their own colors. All five women stand up, and in a few minutes one woman raises her hand and correctly names her color. What is it and how did she know?

If you're not sure of the answer, work on it before proceeding.

Once again, the woman correctly identified her hat as black. She reasoned that if hers were white, the four remaining women would be back in the four-woman situation—which they could solve. If you reason through all the steps you should find it intricate and fascinating.

Thanks to E. R. Emmet's *101 Brain Puzzlers* we can present you with an even tougher problem. We're not including the answer because we know you wouldn't work on it if we did. If you're really stumped, write to us.

Five women are wearing hats on their heads taken from a pool of five white, two red, and two black hats. Each is asked to deduce the color of her hat from the colors of the other four hats she can see. Finally one woman says, "I must be wearing a white hat." She's right! How did she figure it out?

You can reason it through if you remember *two* kinds of contraction. The first kind (which we used in the Hundred Artisans in chapter 1) reduces the size of the problem in order to make it more manageable and focused. The second kind (used in the Colored Hats problems above) reduces a problem to smaller elements which are already familiar to you. This procedure is similar to some methods of mathematical proof.

You might try some variations on this Colored Hats problem by using different ratios of colors or even by putting *two* hats on some heads. The possibilities are astounding.

This whole series of problems is reminiscent of Indian Poker, since each player's own element is the only one she doesn't see. The hat problems are really more interesting though, because reasoning does help—the outcome is not based on luck.

As with the Colored Hats puzzle, the outcome of this next game is not based on chance. In this game, the other player often seems necessary only to make mechanical answers. You might be acquainted with the game of Jotto as we present it here. It's even more likely that you recognize its trademarked alter egos, Master Mind and Merlin. In our third chapter we introduce three brand-new games that also build on the basic Jotto theme: Barter, Array, and Secrets.

JOTTO

Equipment: Paper and pencil, and knowledge of five-letter words. (Note: Names and other proper nouns are off limits in all the word games in this book.)

Object: To guess your opponent's hidden word before she guesses yours.

Play: Two people play at once. Each plays offense and defense throughout the game. Each player decides on a five-letter word (*no repeated letters*) to be her hidden element. This should be written on a sheet of paper that remains hidden from the opponent. Offensive moves entail making guesses about your opponent's hidden word, learning from the responses received, and deducing her hidden word. Defense is mechanical and consists of responding to the guesses hazarded about *your* hidden word. The first person to guess the other's word wins.

Offensive guesses take the form of five-letter words (again, no repeated letters). The defensive player must respond by telling how many of the letters in the guessed word are also in her hidden element. When she has made this response, it is her turn to make a guess about her opponent's hidden word.

Both players might write the complete alphabet across the top of their sheets of paper so they can cross off letters as it becomes apparent that the letters are not included in their opponent's hidden element. For the same reason, a good player will carefully keep track of her questions and the responses she gets. A conscientious novice will also keep track of her *opponent's* questions and the obtained answers—so that she knows just what she's already given away. This will allow the novice to see the logic of not just one, but two people, and it will enable her to become a better player.

The following sample game should help you understand these

rules. Actually, it's only *half* a game, since we're only including *one* person's hidden word, the guesses from the other person, and the responses (and commentary, of course).

1. *Guess:* FIGHT, *answer:* 0.

This is about the best answer to get, especially early in the game, since it tells you that these letters are definitely not included in your opponent's word. You can go back to your alphabet and cross these letters out. From now on you can use these as "safe" letters in guesses to find out about *other* letters.

2. *Guess:* CASED, *answer:* 2.

It can be a good idea to try as many new letters as possible in your first few guesses. You can gain a lot of information quickly, and if you are methodical, it can work almost like the chart method of solving the twelve-ball puzzle. Alternatively, you might have guessed a word like OUGHT in order to make use of some safe letters and look for the inevitable vowels in the hidden word.

3. *Guess:* BALED, *answer:* 3.

It's important *not* to assume that only letters in common among the guesses are getting positive responses. Consider the following example from an actual game in which the hidden word was FLAME. The offensive player asked FIGHT, LIGHT, MIGHT, got 1 as a response each time, and was convinced that it had to be the I, G, H, or T. This is a very common mistake—don't make it. (If you think your opponent is closing in on your word, you may have to make this "mistake" consciously, to save a guess—such as FLUME or FLAME, and catch up. Chances are, after all, that it *is* one of the common letters.)

4. *Guess:* DEALS, *answer:* 2.

Since only the B was removed after guess 3 (DEALS contains all of the letters in BALED except the B), and the response went from 3 to 2, B must definitely be in the hidden word.

5. *Guess:* DIALS, *answer:* 1.

Now you know that E is in the word. Since I was a definite "no" from FIGHT in the first guess, and only E was removed after guess 4, you use the same reasoning here as you did to determine B on guess 4, and you find that E must also be in the hidden word. The one positive response in DIALS could be for either D,A,L, or S. (The player might have wasted a guess here. She does not need to be so positive before moving into a new line of guessing.)

6. *Guess:* SLIDE, *answer:* 1.

Since you know from guess 5 that E accounts for the 1, the other 4 letters cannot be in the word, which means, going back to the guess of DIALS, that A is. Now B,E, and A are definite. It is unlikely that there are other vowels to be guessed, so start trying new consonants. You might also rewrite the alphabet at the top of your page to see at a glance which letters you haven't used yet.

7. *Guess:* RINKS, *answer:* 2.

You now know, since I and S are definitely out, that two of the three letters, R,N, and K are in the word. To determine which letter is out, combine two of R,N, and K with the three definite letters —B,E, and A. If you've picked the correct 2 letters, you'll have all 5 and maybe even have guessed the hidden word! If 4 is the response, then you'll need another turn to determine which of the 2 letters just used is contained in the hidden word.

8. *Guess:* BAKER, *answer:* 5.

K and R were tried and were correct. Now all you need to do is a bit of unscrambling.

9. *Guess:* BREAK, *answer:*   You win!

There's quite a bit of luck involved in this game (getting an answer of 4 to your very first guess is a good example), so it's good to play over and over again to even out the odds. The game with words is really superior to Master Mind, which uses colors, because with words the natural limits of the language both help and hinder you but definitely make the game more interesting.

Choosing your hidden word involves a great deal of strategy. Beginners often like to choose words with unusual letters in them, but this can lead to giving too many zero answers, which gives your opponent too much information. Semicommon letters are very good (m's, n's, y's), especially if the word is hard to unscramble (try DEMON sometime). A nasty trick is to choose a word with common letters that might confuse your opponent. If your word is CARES, she may well try SCARE, RACES, and ACRES before she gets to the right combination.†

† Actually, we like to play with a rule that gives you a victory if you make two consecutive guesses that earn answers of "5." Otherwise, words like CARES are too tempting to use and can destroy the real fun of the game. On the other hand, unscrambling can be a real challenge; try, for example, to make a word out of NOTOIL.

If you feel like you're closer to winning than your opponent is, you might deliberately play a little easier (asking words that you know will get 2s instead of 4s). If she catches on to your advanced position she might take lots of chances playing catch-up and might be lucky and beat you to a correct guess. If you play a subtle game for a bit, you might be able to sneak close to winning. If she only has one turn after she realizes you're almost there, she probably won't be able to preempt your victory. In any event, this strategy (never to be articulated) can be good for your friendship.

We're going to offer you some variations on Jotto, two right now and Barter, Secrets, and Array in chapter 3, but *you* can also change the game, of course. Four-letter Jotto is manageable without paper during a long car-trip. Alternatively, making the words longer or allowing repeated letters would certainly increase the challenge. Repeated letters also increase the luck element in the game because you may stumble on letters the other person has used more than once and gain an advantage. This added luck element may or may not be desirable.

DUAL JOTTO

One basic complaint can be registered about Jotto: there isn't enough crucial interaction between the players. Dual Jotto takes care of that. In this variation of the game, the rules are the same as for basic Jotto *except:*

For each word you venture in the quest for your opponent's hidden element, you must also tell her what *your* answer would be if it had been a guess about your own hidden word. In this way your deduction process is constrained by your need to be defensive and not part with too much information that will help your opponent.

Example: If your secret word is MOATS, and your guess is CHAIR, you must also say that CHAIR gets an answer of 1 from your word.

This makes for a *very* tough game. Moreover, it is very difficult to keep track of the available information, so be careful with your answers and write everything down. It's a very good idea, for the first few guesses, to ask words that get a 1 from you. This way, you don't start your opponent off with too much helpful information.

ERROR JOTTO

In this terrifying version, you *must* make one (and only one) error in one of your *responses* during the first five rounds of the game. In standard Jotto this means making an error in response to your opponent's guess. With Dual Jotto you can also make an error when you're reporting what one of your own guesses would get as a response from your own word. Truly frightening.

Here are a couple of great word games that are easy to learn and rapidly addicting. Neither one has any hidden elements but both are wonderfully challenging.

AUTO CROSSWORD

Equipment: Paper and pencil. Draw a 5 by 5 grid. Keep it hidden from your opponent.

Object: To accumulate more points than your opponent.

Play: The two players alternate calling out letters, and both players fill in their grids with each letter as it is called out. The players try to form words vertically and horizontally in crossword fashion. (Right-to-left or bottom-to-top words do not earn points.)

Scoring: three-letter word = 5 points
four-letter word = 10 points
five-letter word = 20 points

Partially overlapping words can both count for points, but a totally contained word does not count. (Example: KEYES counts 15, for KEY plus EYES. LAPEN counts 15, for LAP plus APE plus PEN. OPENS counts 20, but no points are awarded for PENS because it is contained in OPENS. PEARN counts 20, for PEAR plus EARN. EAR doesn't count because it's included in both EARN and PEAR.) If a four- or five-letter word is used twice in one grid then it is worth only half as many points the second time. There is a great advantage to calling the last letter, so players should alternate going first or assign a handicap to make up for it. We often let the first player call out two letters immediately and then have the players alternate.

Here's an example of one person's filled-in board with the point values she earned. Her opponent called the first and second letters and then the even-numbered letters thereafter. This player called all the odd-numbered letters, including the important last one.

(The boxes are numbered here to show you the order in which they were filled.)

Score:

S [3]	T [5]	A [8]	R [9]	S [12]	20
M [1]	E [2]	N [7]	I [6]	B [15]	5+5
A [10]	L [4]	I [24]	M [16]	O [21]	0
C [11]	L [6]	E [14]	A [17]	N [19]	20
K [23]	S [18]	A [22]	T [20]	E [25]	10

Score: 20 20 0 5+5 10

Total: 120
(a slightly better than average score)

Winning the game depends a great deal on planning. For example, you might prepare for the possibility that your opponent will call out a very unusual letter late in the game. (Similarly, you should save room for some strange letters for the end of the game to ruin *her* board.) Working from the upper left hand corner slowly down to the lower right is a good plan, since that's the way words develop anyway. The bottom right square is a perfect place for an S, but keep it a secret!

Here are both players' boards from a second, more advanced, game. You might draw empty grids on your own and follow the play. Again, the small numbers in each little box tell you the order in which the letters were played. The player who finished with 130 points ("Even") began with S and P and then called out the even turns.

Even

Score:

S¹	W¹⁸	E⁶	A⁴	T³	20
P²	R¹⁰	I¹¹	O¹²	R⁷	20
O⁵	Y¹⁹	D²³	R¹⁶	U¹⁵	0
T⁹	E²²	S²¹	T¹³	E¹⁷	10
S⁸	O²⁵	E²⁴	A¹⁴	R²⁰	5

Score: 20   5+5   5   20   20

Total: 130

Odd

Score:

P²	A⁴	R¹⁰	T³	S¹	20
O⁵	R²⁰	E²²	U¹⁵	W¹⁸	5
R⁷	I¹¹	O¹²	T¹³	A¹⁴	10+10
T⁹	D²³	E²⁴	O²⁵	Y¹⁹	0
S⁸	E¹⁷	E⁶	R¹⁶	S²¹	20

Score: 20   10+10   0   20   20

Total: 145

To give you a sense of the end-game strategy that is involved, consider the decision facing "Even" on move 24. Her bottom row across reads S--AR. There is no chance for more points in the third column going down. The second column down could take a T (for YET), S (YES), or N (YEN) for 5 more points. Unfortunately an R does not give 20 (15 more) because one who is more wry is WRIER and not WRYER.

The other empty box—into which this player actually put an E for 5 points (EAR)—could also have taken a B, C, F, J, M, O, P, T, or W for these 5 points (BAR, CAR, etc.). Why the E? It looked like the best chance for more points during move 25. If "Odd" had called a B, D, F, G, N, R, T, or Y, a four-letter word would have materialized (BEAR, DEAR, etc.). An S would be just as well because SEA and YES would give 10 more points. Finally, H, M, P, or W would net 20 points on the bottom row (SHEAR,

SMEAR, etc.). In large part, then, the game was decided on this last call. The O (for TUTOR) did "Even" no good, and she lost, 145 to 130.

As you can see in this last game, many of the moves are defensive. The best games are not always the highest scoring ones because a good player will frequently call a letter that hurts her own score but is meant to cost an opponent even more points. You might try this game on paper napkins in a restaurant.

This next diversion is called simply "The Game" in some households. Make sure you're well rested before you play!

SCRAMBLE

Equipment: The letter tiles from a Scrabble game (leave out the blank tiles)—or make your own.

Object: To have the most tiles at the end of the game, as parts of words that are four letters or more.

Play: The game is best for two to four people. The letter tiles should be turned face down in the middle of the table (*not* in a box or bag).

One person (whoever is conveniently located or nimble-fingered) begins turning over the tiles one at a time so that every player sees the new letter at the same instant. If the "turner" is going too slowly or stops altogether (to think or scratch her head), someone else is permitted to start flipping tiles too. In this way, all the players control the flow of the game. Tiles can be turned over even when words remain to be arranged from the upturned pile in the middle.

All of the players try to make words (of at least four letters) from the tiles. There are two ways to make words:

1. *Mix:* Using upturned letters from the center of the table, a player mentally unscrambles a word, calls it out, and then moves the tiles so that the word is spelled out in front of her. When a word is called, no more tiles are flipped until this word has been arranged in front of the caller.

2. *Steal:* A player can also make a new word by stealing a complete word from another player (or from herself) and adding at least one tile from the middle of the board. A player may not steal a word just to form a variation of it. (Example: BALL to BALLS or FINE to FINED is no good. POTS to STOPPED, or CASE to SCARE is okay.) The stealer must be able to use all the letters in the stolen word.

As you can see, when calling out a word you must be sure to add any prefixes or suffixes that are available at the first opportunity.

For example, if S, A, O, P, T, S are the letters in the pot, then calling out SPOT precludes correcting this call to SPOTS because the latter is merely a variation of the former. On the other hand, SPOT can be "corrected" or stolen by someone else to form POSTS.

Finally, it is also possible to "steal" two separate words to combine them into one, so long as you always include at least one letter from the upturned pile. For example, if VOTE and SALE have already been unscrambled and arranged and an R is upturned, you could call ELEVATORS and acquire all nine letters.

Winning: When all the tiles are used, or no more words can be formed, the game is over. Players get one point for each tile they have acquired (face values of the Scrabble letters are irrelevant).

Notes: A three-player game is best. It's a good idea for beginners to learn together, because it can depress a beginner and bore an advanced player if they play together. It's important to keep the game moving quickly, so it's best to learn to play with quick instinctual reactions rather than slow and painstaking analysis of the options. When in doubt, flip a new tile!

Strategy: It's hard to know whether to concentrate on a steal or take a mix right away. Basically you should think about a steal when the upturned pile (as opposed to those already in front of players) is unbalanced—either mostly consonants or mostly vowels. Planning ahead is very important. You should always know what you'll do with the next S, for example. When two players call the same word at the same time, they cancel each other out, so maybe you should even have *two* possibilities waiting.‡ In other words, if someone already has "liver" in front of her when an S is turned up, you should be ready to call "sliver." This could easily be called by someone else too, though, so be ready to call "silver" and take the word.

Once you start playing the game frequently, you'll become familiar with the words and variations that appear frequently. This readiness is important because in a fast-moving game you must be able to call a word almost as fast as you can see it.

---

‡ If two people call out words of different lengths at the same time, the longer one wins automatically. If the two different words are the same length, perhaps the more elegant or unusual one should win.

Here are a couple of typical word patterns:

vain
      naive ravine
vein

      patio
iota
      ratio

      tapers   parties traipsed
tape paste
      staple   plaster splatter
      (or plates
        or pastel) staples plasters splatters

It is often a good strategy to ignore the letters of a simple word on the table when it's likely the word would be stolen from you anyway. Wait a little while, concentrate on something else, and steal later on. You'll discover other common word combinations and strategies as you play. Good luck!

Many of the games we've studied in this section have incorporated random factors. In the card games, of course, the deal of the cards is random, while in word and guessing games randomness can easily be incorporated in variations. Often in poker a good player is one who can minimize the effect of randomness on her game. The more control she can exercise the better are her chances of winning.

Randomness is not confined to games and is not necessarily undesirable. In many real-life situations, randomness can be the key to attaining greater efficiency through previously unimagined solutions. Consider the following illustration.

BETTER TOLLBOOTHS

Interstate 95 between New Haven, Connecticut, and the New York Thruway is heavily traveled by shoppers, commuters, and long-distance travelers. There are four $.25 tolls set up (at West Haven, Stratford, Norwalk, and Greenwich) along the stretch. Why not just have one toll plaza and collect $1.00? For long-distance travelers this would be fine, but many short-trippers would escape with their change intact. In effect, a single-toll setup would require that some shoppers and commuters subsidize others. If the toll were in Greenwich, near Exit 3, for example, then drivers who live near Exit 40 and work near Exit 10 would use the turnpike heavily and yet pay no tolls. For this reason, the current state of affairs (four tollbooths) is easily enough understood.

Randomness can work wonders in this turnpike situation. Leave all the tollbooths standing and then *randomly* choose a toll plaza each day at which to collect $1.00. The other three plazas can be driven through and large signs will announce that no toll is collected at this location on this day. *On average,* each tollbooth will be used one out of every four days and unused the other three. Alternatively, randomly choose a plaza at which to charge $1.25 and, on average, every fifth day have no toll at all. The slight advantage of this system is that even after passing three free toll stations, a driver cannot be sure that there is a toll ahead that might be worth avoiding.

The benefits of this tollbooth plan are enormous. The labor required to collect $1.00 or $1.25 is no more than that employed to collect twenty-five cents. In fact, $1.00 is probably collected more quickly because fewer drivers will need to receive change. Thus more than three-fourths of the labor currently used can be employed more efficiently elsewhere. There will also be tremendous savings of driver-time because the traffic will need to stop and form lines just *once* along the highway and not four times.

Notice how important it is for the flexibility to be random. Only half of the solution involves raising toll revenues by less frequent but higher charges at different locations. The other part of the plan is to randomize the daily selection of the toll's location. If not for this randomness, many drivers would soon go to the trouble of exiting before the toll plaza and using local roads to save the dollar. Luckily, few people find this profitable at $.25 an excursion.

It is true that CB radios might keep drivers informed of where the active tollbooths are located. However, this is probably no great problem. Many CB-ers joined the cult to avoid smokies (police) because they value their time highly and prefer to exceed the speed limit. These drivers will not find it worthwhile to leave the turnpike and fight local traffic lights in order to avoid a highway toll.*

Does this use of randomness appeal to you? Many other aspects of games can also be successful when incorporated into real-life situations, as you'll see later on in this chapter. Meanwhile, here's another example of randomness in problem solving.

RANDOM INFORMATION

A serious illustration of randomizing involves the telephone system. The heavy use of "information," or directory assistance, presents problems that are, by now, familiar. Rising labor costs have elicited a variety of responses from the phone companies and regulatory bodies. For example, New York and Virginia now charge for each of these calls (beyond a certain number), Connecticut adamantly forbids such charges, and California does not charge but does discourage the lazy and impatient users by playing a recorded announcement that reminds the customer to use the printed listings whenever possible. Defenders of free information

---

* Furthermore, frequent users could continue to purchase passes or coupons, which substantially reduce the actual toll. In this manner, out-of-staters pay a higher charge and constant travelers would have even less reason to go the CB route.

calls argue that many senior citizens and handicapped people cannot manage to use the directories.

These facts allow for a neat solution. Add to the now popular 411 (or equivalent) information number an additional number like 511. Similarly, 555-1313 could be a "deluxe" partner of 555-1212, the number for out-of-area directory assistance. When callers dial 411, they would be greeted with a recording that says that 411 is a "slow" information number, while 511, at a charge, will get immediate service. (Another feature might erase any 511 charge if the caller is kept waiting more than four rings, or if the number she desires is unavailable.) In this manner, customers can choose whether or not to pay for the service. The wait at 411 will be substantial enough to make it quicker to use the telephone book than to opt for the free service. Of course, most of the elderly and handicapped will not mind the delay because they prefer the free information service. The phone company will gain some income from 511 and won't have to employ as many operators for 411 service.

The problem with this plan concerns certain callers who will dial 411 and then go about chores as they become familiar with the length of the instituted delay. Here again, randomizing will perfect the plan. Sometimes, the information assistant will answer 411 quickly, and sometimes there will be a two-minute delay (or so). On average, the random† delay will be such that it will be to a hurried caller's advantage to use the book when this alternative is available. Once again an annoying inefficiency can be corrected by applying a little randomness.

While we're on the subject of telephones, here's an obnoxious telephone game that can keep you amused for quite some time. Find a partner who likes to laugh, and play it sometime when you're bored.

† This may not be quite random. There is no reason why the delay cannot be a function of the availability of phone company personnel (who may be busy with 511 calls).

AREA CODES

Equipment: Working telephone (and an extension phone if possible), a phone book, and a telephone company that hasn't read this book.

Object: To guess which state your opponent has called on the phone.

Play: Two people play. The first player looks in the phone book and chooses a state to call. She dials the area code of that state plus 555-1212. (A push-button phone is good because the second player can't get any hints from overhearing the dialing pattern.) This number will give her "information." She hands the phone to the second player and then listens on the extension, if there is one.

The second player talks to the information assistant as long as she needs to (or can), and then has three chances to guess which state has been called. If she guesses correctly on the first try, she gets five points. Second try is three points and third is one point.

There are a few rules and suggestions about what the second player can't (or should) say on the phone. She may not ask outright what state it is, nor should she mention any state names. (This makes it too easy. Chances are if she says, "I'd like a number in New York please," the operator will say something like, "I'm sorry, but you called Minnesota information.")

The operator's accent is the biggest clue, so engaging in conversation is good strategy. Many states in the country have cities named Columbus or Columbia, so this is often a good start. After that, a common name and street address (the four most popular streets in the country: Main, Elm, Maple, and First) can be helpful. A chatty manner doesn't hurt either. But don't play this game too often or all our phone bills will go up!

Are you interested in some telephone trivia? How many telephone numbers do you think there are in one area code? Common sense would tell you that 7 positions (each with 10 possible numbers) means 10^7 possibilities, or 10,000,000. Actually, the number is quite a bit smaller than this.

The first digit cannot be a 0 because that would signal the operator. It also can't be a 1, which would indicate a nonlocal call in many states. Similarly, the second digit cannot be a 0 or 1 because both of these are clues to the phone company that an area code has been dialed. Now the total quantity of numbers is reduced to $8 \times 8 \times 10^5$, or 6,400,000. Beyond even this you've got to substract some more possibilities because some exchanges are for phone booths or telephone company offices.

This doesn't leave that many numbers per area code, which can be a problem. Consider the example of New York City. The population is close to 9,000,000, and if the average family size is 3, there must be a minimum of 3,000,000 residence phones. Now add *business* phones (and remember all the people who commute into New York to work). It seems that they should have run out of phone numbers already, doesn't it?

It's no wonder the phone company encourages businesses to add extensions rather than new lines. Once upon a time, calling long distance information required only the area code and 555 and any four digits (not 555-1212 necessarily). Any four numbers for the final digits would still get you information. With the number situation now, however, there's not as much extra space in the phone system, so you'd better dial the correct number.

We firmly expect to have phone numbers increased by one digit soon—or, perhaps, the area codes will have to be redivided and increased in number. A less dramatic (but partial) solution that the phone company in New York has already adopted is to require a caller to dial 1 before an out-of-area number.

Apart from telephones, we are particularly fond of elevators (as you saw in our discussion of Scramble), so we're including discussions of elevator problems to bring in an old theme. The first (thanks to Russell L. Ackoff's *The Art of Problem Solving*) is a very good example of expansion being used to solve a real-life problem.

ELEVATOR PATIENCE

The tenants of a large office building began to complain to the manager about the long wait for elevator service. Some were so vehement that the manager started to worry that they'd leave the building. She called in a team of experts to help her solve her elevator problem.

These experts suggested installing faster elevators or adding new elevators to increase the total number. The manager knew that these suggestions entailed great expense and could not be justified by the earnings of the building. She had to make her tenants content with the elevator system, but she couldn't afford to make major changes.

Finally a young personnel psychologist spoke up. The psychologist's solution was eventually acclaimed by everyone, and though simple and relatively inexpensive, it stopped the complaints.

What was her answer? Think before proceeding.

The solver reasoned that people complained about slow elevator service because they were bored while they waited and therefore conscious of the passing time. The psychologist suggested that walls of full-length mirrors be installed on the face of every elevator bank. Tenants could entertain themselves by watching themselves and each other (surreptitiously, of course) in the mirrors.

It's a marvelous solution to the problem. Do you see the expansion? Instead of simplifying or changing the existing problem, the psychologist went beyond the stated limits to the problem and found something *else* wrong. She didn't remove something from the equation to solve it, she added an entirely new element. Needless to say, this solution is now familiar in other contexts such as the recorded music we hear when waiting for an airline agent to answer the telephone.

Our second bit on elevators is a good example of the many wonderful puzzles that need to be investigated in the everyday world around us. Where do elevators rest? How can we minimize waiting time (not just *perceived* waiting time, which mirrors can take care of)?

You should study the patterns of elevator banks in skyscrapers. Frequently a built-in feature sends the elevator back to the lobby when the elevator is not in use—especially in residential buildings. This is sensible from a safety point of view, since a tenant pursued into the building will find a ready elevator.

Elevators are called from the lobby half the time, while any single other floor is a much rarer calling point. For example, if one elevator handles floors 11 through 20, then half of the calls for that elevator are from the lobby and $\frac{1}{20}$ of the calls are from each nonlobby floor (11 through 20). If we are interested in minimizing the total waiting time then perhaps the elevator should return to a point *between* the lobby and the eleventh floor. The location of such a point depends on the time function we seek to minimize.‡ Perhaps this is best pictured approximately: The "average" call to go down comes from between the 15th and 16th floors, so maybe the elevator should wait halfway between *this* point and the lobby, or between the 7th and 8th floors.

The problem is more complicated when, as is typical, there is more than one elevator servicing a given set of floors. You might think about this problem one day. Furthermore, a really sophisticated system (in which time is *really* valuable), would place the elevators in different spots at different times of day—closer to the lobby in the morning, and so forth.

Moving from elevators to frozen fish, here's an excellent example of the use of expansion to solve a real-life problem (again, thanks to Russell L. Ackoff).

Frozen food was an expanding industry in England after World War II, because refrigerator-freezers were just becoming common in individual homes. One food company decided to market frozen fish to cash in on the new market.

Initially sales were good, but they dropped off quickly because the fish tasted flat. Apparently the fish underwent chemical changes while they were stored on ice in the boats. The company decided to transport the fish *live* in big tanks until they got to the docks and could be frozen. Still the fish did not taste fresh. Chemists discov-

‡ You may have noticed that this is similar to the question in chapter 1, of where the first shoe store should open up on a straight line.

ered that the fish underwent the taste change even while living in the tanks because they didn't move around enough.

While many scientists were trying to find ways to keep the fish moving by rotating the water, someone knowledgeable in the natural history of fish observed the experiments. This observer made an offhand suggestion that solved the problem quite easily. What was the expansion-oriented solution?

The suggestion was that a predator be put in the large tanks of fish to keep the fish swimming. Although some fish were devoured, the better taste and added sales more than made up for the lost fish!

Once again by stepping outside the boundaries of a problem, it is solved simply. Instead of asking (as the scientists did) what artificial device might keep the fish moving, the solver looked at the larger picture to see why the fish moved under normal circumstances.

Just to keep you sharp, here is a quick one back on the shore: Do you know why manhole covers are round? (Think about this seriously.)

Manhole covers are round because it's the only workable shape where the cover *can't* fall through the hole.

LOOSE ENDS

It's time to move on to some new material, but to keep your puzzle-solving skills honed, here's another challenge:

MATCHSTICKS

Moving just *two* matchsticks, change the figure below from five square boxes to four.

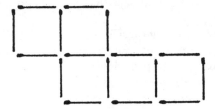

You probably came up with a solution like the one below (which is not bad).

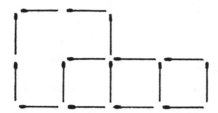

Here's a tougher condition: Move two matchsticks (from the original configuration) to make four boxes, *each the same size.*

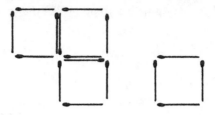

If you came up with this one (or a variation), you're pretty sharp.

Now, still moving only two matchsticks, try making four equal-size boxes with *no* shared or double walls.

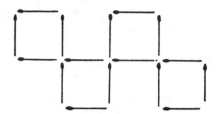

Voilà! This is an elegant solution. The trick is to count the sixteen matchsticks and realize that to make four equal boxes with no double walls requires making the four boxes separately—with no shared walls.

Doing this problem should make you realize that contraction and expansion can't solve everything. Your common sense can come in handy too.

Are you ready for another telephone game? Here's an easy one that's reminiscent of The Price is Right.

THE TELEPHONE BOOK GAME

Equipment: Telephone book (big city books are good).

Object: To make the closest estimate of how many of a given last name will be listed in the phone book.

Play: Any number can play. Players take turns calling out last names, and then everyone guesses how many of that name will be listed. Guesses can be either in terms of numbers or columns.

Discussion: You can see how easy the basic concept of the game is, but there are twists to it that keep it interesting. Using ethnic names can yield quite different results in different cities, for instance. It's a good idea to find out approximately how many names are in a column, since it will save time when counting up the names to determine the winner.

You've come to the end of our section on puzzles and diversions. Our next chapter is full of brand new games to play. It may seem at first as if you've entered a realm entirely removed from puzzles, but before long you will discover many elements that are common to both games and puzzles.

3

New Games and Strategies

Games that require players to form lines with their pieces or occupy more board area than their opponents include some of the most popular pastimes in history. This popularity is probably surpassed only by related games, in which pieces are moved and areas are controlled as means toward specific ends such as wiping out opposing pieces or capturing certain spaces or objects. The entire set of these games might be called "space" games. The group includes Tic-Tac-Toe, Go, Nine-men's Morris, Hex, Sipu, Checkers, Chess, and newer games like Stratego and Othello.

The true gamesperson deserves entire volumes on each of these games. For our purposes, it is interesting to observe a common theme in these games: there is no hidden element. All the options are clear and "on the table." Apart from psychological factors, the game turns on strategy and the ability of the players to think ahead. While foresight is a part of every game, it is the *central* feature of space games because so many other strategic elements are removed. There is no reward for recalling past moves, and guessing skills are not involved.

It is easy for even the simplest of these games to remain exciting, though they may be played on small boards and with familiar opponents. This continuing excitement results from the fact that with some analysis and imagination the players can agree on rule changes, thereby inventing new games.

The tac-toe group of games is a convenient term for those space games played with marks (like X and O) that are *not* moved once placed on the board. Simple Tic-Tac-Toe, of course, is overly familiar. Played on a 3 by 3 board, the game can always be forced to a draw. In all the extensions of this game, the reader should consider the many possibilities for rule changes. These include: required starting spots, extra moves as a bonus or compensation, variable board sizes, and weighted objectives (2 points for some accomplishment or configuration and 1 point for another). As with all games, the general idea should be that a good game allows superior analysis to win. Neither side should have too clear an advantage, and the game should be too complicated to analyze perfectly.

Super-Tac-Toe and Duper-Tac-Toe are the results of rule changes. Each can easily be altered further to suit your taste.

SUPER-TAC-TOE

Equipment: Paper and pencil. A 5 by 6 drawn grid is a good starting board.

Object: To occupy more spaces than your opponent.

Play: Two players alternate placing their marks, X or O, in the boxes of the grid. In this version, X goes first, but his first move cannot be in one of the centermost 6 boxes. (This tends to eliminate the advantage of going first and adds to the strategic possibilities.) When a player forms a 3-in-a-row (called 3row hereafter), he is awarded an extra move. However, no player may ever form a 4-in-a-row (4row). The game ends when the boxes are filled or when any further move would require making a 4row. If one player has no more legal moves available, the other player can continue to mark in boxes until the boxes are all filled or any further moves would violate the rules.

	A	B	C	D	E	F
1		X_{4c}				
2	X_4	X_1	X_3	O_3		
3		X_2	O_1	O_{3a}		
4	X_{4a}	O_2	X_{4b}			
5						

Moves by X and O are numbered to ease following the game. X may not begin in C2, C3, C4, D2, D3, or D4. O_3 in D2 gives O an extra move because of his 3row. A5 and E1 are now forbidden moves because they would create 4rows. O's extra move, O_{3a}, is in D3, an offensive placement. X_4 earns X an extra move, in A4. This, in turn, gives him X_{4b} and then X_{4c}. The completed game board appears as follows:

	A	B	C	D	E	F
1	O_7	X_{4c}	X_{5a}		X_6	O_6
2	X_4	X_1	X_3	O_3	X_{5b}	X_7
3	X_5	X_2	O_1	O_{3a}	X_{4d}	O_{5b}
4	X_{4a}	O_2	X_{4b}	O_4	O_{4a}	O_5
5		X_{6a}	O_{5b}		O_{5c}	O_{5a}

After O_7, neither player can move into D1, A5, or D5 without violating the 4row rule. The game is over. X occupies 14 spaces and O has 13; X wins. Go ahead and play!

Discussion: In the game played above there are a good number of controversial moves, and the example is not meant to demonstrate expert play. X_3 might have been in B1 to form 3row and earn a bonus move, but X felt that a move toward the middle was advisable. As you can see, the B3, B2, B1 row did not close up, and X_{4c}, arguably, did the job. Many other decisions could be questioned; the best moves in this game are not obvious.

Of course there are many ways to analyze Super-Tac-Toe. Contraction, as usual, may help a good deal. Analysis of a 4 by 4 board (ignoring the rule that requires the first move to be noncentral) will clarify the power of diagonals, crossed diagonals, and the danger of confinement. Experimentation will show you the meanings of these terms. Crossed diagonals are demonstrated below. B3 is now vastly superior to other O_2 options:

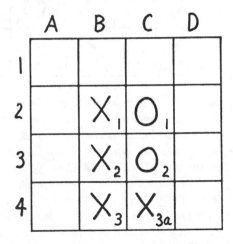

What is the best O_3 move in the game below?

If it's C_1, then what next for O_{3a}? "Confinement" refers to the result of an O_3 and O_{3a} that keep O in lines C and D. Planning ahead at this stage involves judging whether lone marks in distant rows will be wasted or will keep you from being confined to less than half the board, and certain defeat.

Finally, it is important to plan within the framework of the 4-in-a-row rule (which prohibits 4rows). Allowing your opponent to form 3 by 3 or similar strongholds almost ensures your victory:

	A	B	C	D	E	F
1		O_{7a}	O_{3a}	O_7		O_6
2	O_{7b}	X_1	X_{3a}	X_{4d}	O_1	X_{4e}
3	O_8	X_{4b}	X_2	X_{4c}	O_2	O_4
4	O_9	X_{4a}	X_4	X_3	O_3	O_5
5		O_{9a}	O_{10}	O_{11}		X_5

The pattern before O_4 demonstrates that only column F is now open to X. O_4 breaks up any further bonus moves for X. After O_6 there is not a spot on the board permissible to X. X now has 11 spaces and the only question is whether O can fill this many before he, too, runs into the rule about 4rows. Clearly, his job is easy. O wins 15 to 11. O might have done even better by first going to column F instead of E.

The lesson of this example is that while there is obvious value to central moves, this value is surprisingly nonoffensive. In fact, clustering can be fatal. The key moves in the game above were O_4, O_5, and O_6. Once O realizes the situation, the race is for spaces in F. The other spaces will never disappear because X is stymied in lines A, 1, and 5.

DUPER-TAC-TOE

Equipment: Paper and pencil. A 5 by 5 or 6 by 6 board is a good start.

Object: To score the most points. One point is awarded for each 3row, 3 points for each 4row, and 5 points for any 5row.

Play: Two players alternate, drawing X or O. The fairest rules forbid the first move from occupying one of the central squares. (There are nine central squares in the 5 by 5.)

	A	B	C	D	E
1		X_1			
2		X_4	X_2		
3		X_3	O_1	O_2	O_3
4		O_4			
5					

O_2 was a poor move. Because the player ignored the value of crossed diagonals, O_4 was necessary after X_4 to block a costly 4row. Now X_5 in D2 guarantees X a 4row at A2 or E2. O_2 in D2 or B2 would have been superior. The remainder of the game is presented on the following page.

	A	B	C	D	E
1	O_{11}	X_1	X_{10}	X_{11}	O_7
2	X_6	X_4	X_2	X_5	O_5
3	X_9	X_3	O_1	O_2	O_3
4	O_9	O_4	X_7	O_{10}	O_6
5	X_{12}	O_{12}	X_{13}	X_8	O_8

Note that X_8 in D5 gains 2 points (4row rather than 3row), but also loses 2 points because placement in E5 would have blocked a 5row for O. O_9 blocks A4, which would have given X a 3row (A2, A3, A4) and a guaranteed 4row. Final score: X wins, 10 to 7.

This is a great game for quick doodling, but be sure to look horizontally, vertically, and in both diagonal directions when scoring. Feel free to vary the board size and other rules.

The most interesting thing about Duper-Tac-Toe is the ease with which exciting variations can be concocted. Quite easily, the board can be expanded, the scoring changed, the players handicapped, and randomness introduced.

The game can also be adapted to three players. Strategy then includes forcing one opponent to block the other opponent. This new game is created by changing the rules so that a 4row is an immediate win (thus forcing some blocks), or by playing a few games and totaling the scores (perhaps with betting so that it's better to finish second than last). We call the three-person variation Triple-Tac-Toe. It's discussed in this chapter after the game of Barter, because Barter develops some principles of three-person games. There's no reason, however, why you can't try a three-person version before reading the Triple-Tac-Toe explanation.

Duper-Tac-Toe itself can be analyzed in a variety of ways. One possibility is to concentrate on the premium given for a 4row. Can a 4row always be blocked? What if a 4row were an automatic win (or the premium were huge) and no credit were given for a 3row?

	A	B	C	D	E
1		X_1			
2			X_2	O_2	
3			O_1	X_3	
4		X_4			O_3
5					

The game above was played with this variation.

X_3 forces O_3. Now, X_4 must go somewhere on the A5–E1 diagonal or O_4 in B4 will lead to a win (two open ends). (Note that B4 is not the only X_4 possibility, i.e., X_4 in E1 allows X_5 in A5 after O_4 in B4.)

After these few moves it becomes clear that only sloppiness will allow an opponent to score a 4row. In a sense, this knowledge lies behind the origin of Duper-Tac-Toe. One's chances for success are improved by looking for 4rows while still scoring points with 3rows.

It should be observed that on a larger board, a 4row becomes possible even if it *is* an automatic win. On a very large board, the first player, playing properly, is assured not only of a 4row but also a 5row.

	A	B	C	D	E	F	G	H
1								
2			X_1					
3				X_2				
4				O_1				
5								
6								
7								
8								

Above is an 8 by 8, with X_1 forbidden in rows 3 through 6 of D and E. There are many options now. But O_2 cannot go in E4, for example, because X_3 in C4 is a winner. (X will win by occupying C3, E2, or B5, forming a 3row with two open ends.) We know a bit about diagonals, so C3 appears to be better than C4 or a more defensive move. But now X_3 in E4 will lead to a win! Thus the temporary key would be for O_1 to be diagonal to X_1, as in the following game.

	A	B	C	D	E	F	G	H
1								
2	O_3	X_3	X_1	X_2	O_2			
3			O_4	O_1	X_5			
4			X_4	X_6		O_5		
5								
6								
7								
8								

Here, O will try E2 for his second move. After X_6, O is finished. He cannot block both line 4 *and* diagonal A7–G1. Where was O's error? O_4?

We have strayed rather far off the main course at this point. The reader may wish to ponder whether it is true that X can always get a 4row once the board is expanded to give him moving space. Of course if X *is* advantaged, we might further constrict his opening move or give O a bonus move at some point. It is easy enough to say that the situation is complicated and big playing areas are difficult to analyze. The point is that the game is vastly improved by letting players strive for 4rows while they get credit for 3row formations. The remaining variable is to weight these two goals. The weighting

(3 to 1) included in the rules of Duper-Tac-Toe is somewhat arbitrary and a result of the authors' experience.

Remember that three-player versions are discussed later in this chapter.

ARRAY

In chapter 2 we discussed the game of Jotto at some length. If you skipped over it you might like to see that material before proceeding with Array. Jotto calls for each player to deduce his opponent's hidden five-letter word by offering five-letter words as guesses and learning from the responses received. Each response indicates the number of letters in the guess that also appear in the hidden word.

Master Mind is a popular trademarked game that is quite similar to Jotto, but colors are used instead of letters and responses distinguish between colors guessed with the correct placement and those guessed correctly but in the wrong order. We prefer Jotto to Master Mind because in Jotto the guesser is constrained by the English language. An additional element of gaming is involved because some letters appear in many words and others do not. Some *combinations* of letters occur more frequently than others.

The basic game can also be altered in many ways. The hidden element might be a five-digit number, for example. This would make playing time a bit longer than in a Master Mind game because the latter uses fewer than ten colors. In fact, an electronic game, Merlin, that we recommend highly (especially for ten- to fifteen-year-olds) plays such a game with nine numbers.

Array is an improvement on this concept because two players' games are now intertwined in a manner reminiscent of Dual Jotto. Apart from the excitement of multidimensional guessing (the hidden element is a 5 by 5 grid of numbers), certain information is only obtainable by *trading* similar information about your *own* hidden element, which your opponent is intent on discovering.

Equipment: Paper and pencil.

Object: Two players are trying to guess each other's 5 by 5 array of numbers.

Start: Each player completes a 5 by 5 array using the digits 0 through 9. For each (horizontal) row and (vertical) column, you must tell the other player the "modular 9." This requires adding up the numbers in that row or column, dividing by 9, and announcing the remainder (in whole numbers, no fractions), or the "mod 9," to your opponent.* (The mod 9 of a series of numbers can also be determined by adding the numbers and then adding together the digits of the sum until only one digit remains.)

Play: Each player takes turns asking for information about the other's array. There are three types of questions that can be asked:

1. *Content information:* You specify a row or column, and state a five digit sequence. The other player will tell you how many of those digits are somewhere in the corresponding hidden row or column.

> *Examples:* You guess 12345; hidden is 36427; answer "3"
> You guess 11227; hidden is 11188; answer "2"
> You guess 34353; hidden is 13278; answer "1"

There are two other types of questions you may ask. These call for "positional" and "individual" information but are used less frequently because each requires you to give up information about your own hidden array.

2. *Positional information:* Instead of the basic content query, you may ask for positional information about your *previous* content guess. Your opponent will tell you how many of the digits you correctly identified were also in the correct position in the five-digit sequence.

> *Example:* You guessed 12345; hidden is 17825; the content answer would be "3," the positional answer, "2."

In return for this information, you *must* give positional information concerning the other player's latest content guess for which your answer was 3 or more. If none exists, or your opponent has already received positional information, he may choose any other previous content guess for which he now desires positional information.

3. *Individual information:* Instead of asking for content or positional information, you may ask about a specific box. Your opponent will tell you the exact contents of the box you specify. In return, you *must* reveal the contents of your own corresponding box.

---

* What if the numbers add up to less than nine? Say, for example, their total is 5. Since 5 divided by 9 is 0 (remember, no fractions), your response would be "5," which is the remainder.

Individual information can only be requested *three times* in each game (by each player).

Winning: If you think that you have deduced the entire array, then you may use your turn to read aloud this deduced array. If it is correct, you have won. If it is not correct, play continues, and you lose your next turn. The first person to correctly deduce his opponent's array is the winner.

	A	B	C	D	E
F	0	1	2	3	4
G	5	6	7	8	9
H	0	1	2	3	4
I	5	6	7	8	9
J	0	1	2	3	4

Example: Above is an example of a hidden array. We must now tell our opponent the mod 9 of each line. For A, we add the column: $0 + 5 + 0 + 5 + 0 = 10$. In mod 9, $10 = 1$ (divide by 9 and look at the remainder, or add the two digits together). For B: $1 + 6 + 1 + 6 + 1 = 15$, and the mod 9 is 6. The mod 9 results for the lines are $A = 1$, $B = 6$, $C = 2$, $D = 7$, $E = 3$, $F = 1$, $G = 8$, $H = 1$, $I = 8$, and $J = 1$.

Discussion: The mod 9 feature is not absolutely necessary, but it adds a strategic element and does shorten the game somewhat. Of course you could also play on a 4 by 4 grid. Individual box information might then be limited to one or two per person in a game. Note that if both players use their three individual requests, *six* boxes are discovered directly because the "asker" must also reveal the contents of this space on his own array.

Strategy: Try to utilize the mod 9 information, and be on the lookout for repeated digits. You might ask 12345 and on the next turn try 67890. If the sum of the responses is less than five, you know that at least one number is being repeated (since the opponent must have *something* in the five boxes). You might next try 11122.

Suppose we are told that the mod 9 of column A is 3. We ask 12345 and the response is 2. 67890 gets a response of 3. Therefore there are no duplicates to worry us. 11122 yields 0. This means that two of the digits 3, 4, 5 are in A (since 12345 got a 2). We could try each separately. 11113 gets a 0, so there must be both 4 and 5 in the hidden column.† Now, of the three remaining unknowns we need to find only two, because mod 9 information will fill in the rest. Therefore, try 45167, which yields a response of 4. We know now that 4, 5, 6, and 7 are in the hidden line. These add to 22 = 4 in mod 9. Since the mod 9 of the line is 3, the missing number is 8 (4, 5, 6, 7, 8 add to 30 = 3 in mod 9). In five guesses we know the *content* of A. We are set to use positional requests along with information from lines F through J to help place positions in A.

If the hidden line contains duplicates, the content requests are tougher. Imagine that we seek to learn about B (mod 9 = 7). 12345 yields a 2, while 67890 yields a 2 as well. We know there is one repeat. 11122 yields a 0. Again, two of the digits 3, 4, 5 are in B. 11223 yields a 1, and 11224 also a 1. Therefore 3 and 4 are in B. We can use 3 and 4 as "knowns" and 1 and 2 as "known absents."‡ 67341 yields a 3, so either 6 or 7 is in B. Try 62341 (yields 3), so 6 is our answer. Similarly, test 8 and 9 (and learn about 0). 34689

---

† There's a tremendous amount of strategy behind all these moves. If we do all of this, then next time we play this opponent he will know to put in a 3 and slow us down a turn in finding out about a 4 or 5. On the other hand, he might not, thinking that we're thinking he will. On the other hand, he might think that we think he thinks . . .

‡ Note the interesting parallel to the logic of the twelve-ball puzzle in chapter 1. Information is obtained by first knowing some information *not* of direct interest to the solver. Similarly, in simple Jotto, the best response to get is a 0, since this lets you use many "safe" letters in requests that can narrow in on the information sought.

gives a 4, and 34619 gives a 4. The four digits are 3, 4, 6, and 9. These add to 22 = 4 in mod 9, so it is 3 that is duplicated.

Do not be fooled (by the length of this process) into thinking that repeats should be widely used in your hidden array. After all, although the content of a line is more difficult to discover when there are repeats, your opponent must also uncover positional information and repeats can minimize or even eliminate (as when you use 55555) this task.

The use of positional requests involves offensive and defensive considerations. If the opponent is likely to ask a positional question on his next turn (as he might when you have just replied "5" to a content request), you might *now* ask a content question concerning a line about which you would appreciate the positional information that your opponent must supply after he asks *his* positional question.

Notes: If you wish to quicken the game but still play on a 5 by 5, you might play with numbers 1 through 7 only. Notice, too, the ease with which handicapping is possible. The better player can offer to skip every nth turn, be subject to more than three individual requests, and so forth. This is a great game for train rides and long waits. Enjoy!

BARTER

Barter is a sophisticated and somewhat complicated game. It can be played by three or more people and has elements of guessing and puzzle games (like Jotto and Array) as well as the collusive aspects of many multiplayer games. It is worthwhile to concentrate on understanding the detailed rules before you begin to play.

Equipment: Paper and pencil. You'll need several smaller slips of paper as well.

Object: The first player to accumulate 50 points is the winner. (Advanced players might play for 80 or more points.) The winner announces when 50 is reached, and then records are inspected.

Start: 1. Each player represents a country. We can call them Aay, Bee, and Cee. Each country produces a different "commodity" or "product," which we can call A, B, or C (ale, bread, and cars, for example). A is made in country Aay, and so forth. Points are awarded for accumulating the output of *other* countries. Three points are given for each of the first ten pieces from any country and then one point for each additional unit. (For example, player Aay gets points for acquiring Bs and Cs. Aay could win with 12 Bs, and 6 Cs: 10 Bs $\times$ 3 = 30 points. Additional Bs are worth one point each: 2 Bs $\times$ 1 = 2, for 32 points. Additionally, 6 Cs $\times$ 3 = 18, for the required 50 points.)

2. As, Bs, and Cs are made by combinations of "factors" s, t, and w (could be steel, timber, and water). Each player *secretly* constructs his country's combination (secret production function) such that the sum of the factors used for one product equals 15, and some of each factor is used. (Player Aay may decide that each A is made with 6s + 4t + 5w [6 + 4 + 5 = 15]. Every factor must be used, so 10s + 5t + 0w is not permitted.)

Play: Choose who goes first and play then proceeds clockwise. A given turn *may* consist of up to three parts (although the latter two parts are frequently passed up) that must be carried out in order.

PART ONE: Players acquire products by sending factors to other countries. This shipment is made *publicly*. At least 15 factor pieces *must* be sent to *each* of the other countries on each turn. The country on the receiving end then sends back, *secretly* on a piece of paper, the number of products that those factors were able to make according to his secret production function. Each country begins with 50 of each factor (s, t, w) but loses and acquires them as they are sent to and received from other countries.

This may seem complicated, so here are some examples. It's Aay's turn. He sends 7s-7t-7w to Cee. (Each player keeps a running tally of his factors. Aay now has 43 remaining of each factor.) Cee's secret production function is 8s + 2t + 5w = 1C. 7s-7t-7w therefore makes *no* Cs (not enough steel), and Aay gets back a private slip that says, "7-7-7 buys 0." If Aay sends 8s-7t-7w, this buys one C, as would 15s-500t-500w (although of course Aay doesn't have so many factors to ship over).

Naturally, 8s-2t-5w buys one C, and 16s-4t-10w buys two Cs—extremely efficiently. The quicker Aay discovers or guesses Cee's secret formula the fewer factors Aay wastes in trying to accumulate Cs.

PART TWO: In the course of a game, a player may trade *factors* directly with another player up to four times.

Thus Aay may tell Bee, "I'll give you 20s and 6t for 9w." Bee accepts or makes a counteroffer and the two players may reach an agreement. An offer, if accepted, cannot be rescinded. Products (commodities) may not be traded in this direct manner.

PART THREE: A country may also acquire a factor by buying from an artificial bank. The "price" is set at one of *each* of the other two factors or three of one other factor. Thus 2s can be bought by "paying" 2t + 2w, *or* by paying 6t (or 6w).

(Note that factors, somewhat unrealistically, do not get used up when they make a product. Whether your shipment of factors buys something or not, the other country adds these factors to its stockpiles. The total supply of each factor in the game as a whole changes only to the extent of the transactions with the bank.)

Summary of Rules: These rules are extensive, so here's a review and some comment. You need the products of other countries to win. These are acquired by sending factors to the other countries and receiving products in return, according to a production formula known only to the other country/player.

Factors are acquired in four ways: (1) Players begin with 50s, 50t, and 50w each. (2) Players acquire factors because factors are sent over by other countries in the quest for products. (3) Factors can also be accumulated by trading with other countries. Products can *not* be sent in trades. (4) Factors can be purchased: 1s + 1t buys 1w, and so forth. 3s or 3t also buys 1w.

Initial Comments: Obviously, if you can deduce another country's formula it becomes easier to acquire that country's product. The formula is deduced in two ways. First, you vary the combinations that you send over and study the results. For example, let's say you are Aay. If 7s-7t-7w gets 1B and on your next turn 4s-7t-7w buys 0B, you know that Bee's formula begins with 5s, 6s, or 7s. If it later turns out that Bee's formula must include exactly 3t, you can deduce that either 7w, 6w, or 5w is correct, since the three coefficients must total 15.

The second way to learn about Bee's formula is from Cee's questions! While you do not see the responses Bee gives Cee, Cee is unlikely to spend too many factors fooling you. As you will see, toward the end of the game the players will race to send factors abroad in return for products. They will impatiently wait for factors to come in so that they can be converted into products by the next turn's shipping process. The more Cee can conserve factors now, the more he will be able to race and the less he will need to wait later. On the other hand, as you get close to Bee's formula yourself, be careful not to "overinquire" since each of your inquiries helps Cee.

Here are the early steps of a sample game. Notice that the players should keep track of their factors on a central, public sheet, but commodity totals are kept private because responses remain secret. A discussion of strategy and notes on the play follow the example. You really should read the notes along with the sample game in order to get its true flavor.

SAMPLE GAME OF BARTER

Secret formulas: A = 3s + 9t + 3w
B = 5s + 5t + 5w
C = 7s + 7t + 1w

Round	Player	Current (pre-turn) Factor Ownership			Product Ownership (Secret)	Attempted Trades		
		s	t	w		To Aay	To Bee	To Cee
1.	Aay	50	50	50	0	—	6s6t6w = 1B	6s6t6w = 0C
	Bee	50	50	50	0	7s7t7w = 0A	—	8s8t8w = 1C
	Cee	50	50	50	0	8s8t8w = 0A	6s6t6w = 1B	—
2.	Aay	53	53	53	1B	—	5s6t5w = 1B	8s8t6w = 1C
	Bee	47	47	47	1C	9s6t9w = 0A	—	7s7t7w = 1C
	Cee	50	50	50	1B	5s10t10w = 1A	6s6t5w = 1B	—
3.	Aay	54	55	61	2B,1C	—	5s6t5w = 1B[1]*	8s8t4w = 1C
	Bee	42	46	41	2C	4s9t4w = 1A[2]	—	6s6t6w = 0C
	Cee	54	49	48	1A,2B	4s9t4w = 1A[3]	5s5t5w = 1B[4]	—
4.	Aay	49	59	60	3B,2C	—	5s6t5w = 1B[5]	7s7t5w = 1C[6]
	Bee	42	42	41	1A,2C	3s9t3w = 1A[7]	—	7s7t5w = 1C[8]
	Cee	59	49	49	2A,3B	4s9t4w = 1A[9]	5s6t5w = 1B[10]	—
5.	Aay	44	64	57	4B,3C			
	Bee	42	38	43	2A,3C			
	Cee[11]	64	48	50	3A,4B			

*Coefficient numbers correspond to the numbers of the Sample Game notes,
which follow.

Notes to the Sample Game:
    1. If 5s6t5w buys 1B, Aay knows that Bee's formula must be
5-5-5, 4-6-5, or 5-6-4, since it must sum to 15. If 5-5-5 now gets 1B,
Aay has his answer. But why give Cee this information? Aay should
probably keep to these ratios or even go 6s6t5w.

2. Bee knows that Cee's 8-8-8 shipment seems to have gotten a oA, because Cee went on to ask 5-10-10. Bee knows that Aay's formula is either very unbalanced (see later discussion) or that the t coefficient is greater than 8 (because Cee's first round attempt seems to have failed). The s and w numbers are then 5 or less since a 6 would mean that the remaining factor was not used at all, and this is against the rules. 5-9-5 would, therefore, get a 1A response, but would not teach Bee anything new.

3. Cee can figure that Bee's 9-6-9 in round 2 failed because Bee is now trying something dramatically different in round 3. But Cee's 5-10-10 was successful. Probably, Aay's t coefficient is somewhere in between 6 and 10. The higher it is, the more likely the w coefficient is low. In other words, it's not the w coefficient that was high in Aay's formula, or Bee's second round try would have been successful. But Cee's own first round try of 8-8-8 was unsuccessful. Therefore it's very likely that Aay's t coefficient is 9 or 10. Given that Bee seems to have figured all this out (or made a lucky guess), Cee may as well imitate Bee and see what his next move is. Anyway, Cee already has 1A more than Bee has, so it's up to Bee to be daring. Moreover, Cee's own t coefficient is fairly high and so in the long run Cee is likely to receive more t's than will Bee, who will be hard pressed to come up with enough t's to buy products from both Aay and Cee. Therefore, Cee ought to play it safe and copy Bee, who looks like no threat.

4. Cee understands Aay's logic as in note 1, but winners take chances. The 1B response is, of course, unknown to Aay.

5. Aay will wait to see if Cee repeats 5-5-5. A 5-5-5 or 6-4-5 try by Aay here *could* cost 15 factors while trying to save one now. Any big gain will come later anyway, so why not watch Cee first.

6. From Bee's second and third turns it appears that 7-7-7 bought 1C unless Bee is very shifty. Aay already knows that Cee's formula has 4w or less. 7-7-4 would be safe. 7-7-3 or 7-7-2 would tell Bee that Aay's shipment of 8-8-4 on turn 3 did buy 1C. There's little to gain by giving this away. Perhaps it's time to mislead Bee into thinking that 8-8-4 was unsuccessful.

7. Bee is lowest on factor ownership and hence, if no one takes chances, Bee will lose. So 4-9-4 should not be repeated. Cee knows the response to 4-9-4 because he tried it too. 3-9-3 is risky (adds to

15 exactly, so there's no room for error) but that's just what Bee must do to win.

8. One risk per turn is enough! Aay has experimented with 8-8-4 and is willing to try 7-7-5. Only a really gutsy Aay would try 7-7-5 *knowing* it would fail!

9. Cee knows that Bee is taking chances because Cee can see the factor ownership list. Why not wait and see if Bee repeats 3-9-3? This lethargy is inexpensive for Cee (it costs 1s and 1w at most).

10. No need to tell Aay that 5-5-5 is golden!

11. As the players discover the formulas (or get close), the game turns to one of logistics. One cannot buy large quantities at once because there are limited factors around. Aay, for example, must wait for the factors that will arrive as Bee and Cee buy As.

Discussion: These notes to the sample Barter game display the intricacies of this game. Obviously it's important to keep a straight face at certain times. In the remaining turns, Bee and Cee may well go to the bank to purchase the t's they will need to ship to Aay.

It is pointless to run through the remaining turns for you, because now that you have seen the hidden production formulas it will be difficult for you to believe any direct trades between players. When playing the game, however, remember that you may give away information (but also fool another player) by offering certain trades. An *offer*, if accepted, must be carried through (no bluffing allowed).

A difficult question: What is the best secret formula? Simplistic (but clever) analysis will demonstrate that it can be poor strategy to use very small or large numbers (6-5-4 is better than 12-2-1). There are two reasons for this conclusion. First (using contraction analysis) a lopsided formula is easier to guess because shipments earn a zero response.†

Let's say the coefficients were required to total 5 instead of 15, this assumption, of course, lets us contract and simplify the analysis. The possible formulas are: 311, 221, 212, 122, 113, 131. 322, 232, and 223 are good opening shipments because a product is bought in four of the six possible situations. If 322 is asked and the response is "yes" (1A or whatever), then the formula might be 311, 221, 212,

---

† This is analogous to a zero response in Jotto—more helpful to the guesser than anything else.

or 122. If oA is the response, then only 113 and 131 are left. Asking one of these will finish the job (ignoring the possibility of trying to fool or delay the third player).

If 1A is the response, one more question will *not* finish the job (e.g. 222 answered 1A, still leaves 221, 212, and 122). Thus a formula with an extreme element is easier to guess. The analysis for formulas summing to 15 is quite similar.

There is another drawback to an extremely unbalanced formula. Once the opponents have figured it out, they will be shipping you an unbalanced set of factors. You will then have the burden and expense of making direct trades and/or buying from the bank. You might argue that your opponents will also need to buy in order to come up with all of the factors you have weighted so heavily. However, they can exchange 2 for 1 (1s + 1t for 1w, for example) while you're stuck with all the w's and must give 3 of them for each s or t. Furthermore, to win you had best acquire products from each of the other countries (easier than all from one because after the first ten you get only one point each). Even if the rules were friendlier (2 for 1 instead of 3 for 1) the chances are that one of your opponents would complete the necessary bank purchases before you.

Despite all the musing about the drawbacks of extreme formulas, there is one overriding factor to be considered. If the opponents have read this or thought through the drawbacks of extreme formulas, then one *should* use an extreme formula to fool them. This is a familiar gaming situation in which you think that the opposition will think that you will think . . .‡

Perhaps the only conclusion that is sensible is that when you do teach the game to someone who has not read these pages, you should be aware that unschooled beginners are likely to try an extreme formula. This is especially true if, when giving examples of the instructions. you offer clearly balanced formulas! The likelihood of this tendency cannot be overemphasized.* Good luck!

---

‡ Readers familiar with game theory know that a "correct" strategy is to toss a coin weighted in favor of the "better" formula but allowing some chance of surprise. However, the meaning of "better" is unclear here since you might be risk-seeking.

* This winning "strategy" against novices is analogous to that suggested in chapter 2, for Finger Baseball.

SECRETS

Equipment: Two decks of cards, a pen, and some slips of paper, or the ability to whisper.

Object: To be the first player to be rid of his cards. (If all players still hold cards when the downpile ends, then the player with the fewest cards wins.)

Set-up: Three or four people play. The dealer gives each player six cards. The remainder of the deck (the downpile) is placed face down in the middle of the table. Eight characteristics of playing cards are important in this game: clubs, diamonds, hearts, spades, odd (Three, Five, Seven, Nine, Jack, King), even (Two, Four, Six, Eight, Ten, Queen, Ace), low (Two through Nine), and high (Ten through Ace). Each player selects one of these characteristics to tell—in secret—to the player on his right. Each player now constructs (writes down) a secret pattern of three of the characteristics (no repeats) in any order, *being sure* to include the characteristic given to him by the player on his left. (In the game, each player will have a head start on figuring out the pattern on his right.)

Play: The dealer goes first. Play consists of two types of moves. A player may take one card from his hand and place it in front of any other player. A card is "accepted" if it fits that player's secret pattern. The first card placed in front of him must meet the requirement of the first characteristic in his pattern. Thus, if C's secret pattern is "club, diamond, odd" (he has received one of these from the player to his left, A), and if A, going first, tries the Nine of clubs in front of C, it will be accepted. (C says "accepted.") A and B now know that the first element in C's pattern is clubs, low, or odd. Once a card is accepted, play goes to the next player in clockwise fashion.

If B also tries a card in front of C, we are now dealing with C's *second* element. If B tries the Eight of clubs, C will say "rejected" because it is not a diamond, but the card will stay on the board (read on). Now B must pick a "replacement" card from the downpile and must try to get a card accepted on the board (not necessarily in front of C again). The next card in front of C, however, is still accepted or rejected based on C's second element (diamonds). In other words, play moves on to the next element in a pattern only after the previous one has been fulfilled. Therefore, you should keep accepted cards in front of each player vertically and rejected ones horizontally. All cards are always visible so players can make some deductions later on without becoming confused or being held at the mercy of some memory whiz.

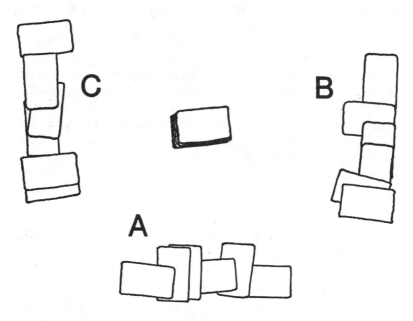

B keeps trying until he places a card that is accepted. After each rejection he picks a replacement card. After an acceptance, but before the next player begins, B (or whoever) must draw penalty cards. He draws one card for each rejection he suffered that turn. His hand will grow correspondingly large as his attempts are rejected. (Remember the object of the game is to have no cards left in your hand.)

After three cards are accepted in front of a player, his pattern repeats itself and other players can begin to reason from previous acceptances and rejections (and from the knowledge that no repeated elements are in any player's secret).

The second type of move allows B to play on his own pile (in front of himself). He *must* play a card that is acceptable according to whichever element of his pattern is now in turn. However, playing on one's own pattern requires the drawing of *two* penalty cards.

Discussion: Note these reasons why B might want to play on his own pattern:

1. B may wish to play on C's secret, but on the *next* element in it, not the one currently at stake. Thus he hopes that A on his next turn will play on C (and be accepted) so that on his own next turn he will face the desired element in C's secret.

2. For strategic reasons, B may want A or C on their next turns to work on an element of B's pattern other than the one now at hand.

3. Toward the end of the game, B may see that A has just one card left in his hand and B may know that A can probably play this card on B to win (it will be accepted), so B plays on himself (suffering the penalties) so that A will be faced with the next element of B's pattern.

Of course the real penalty for playing on one's own pile includes taking two penalty cards and giving up information about one's own pattern, as well as losing the chance on this turn to learn about other players' secrets while getting rid of some cards.

Strategy: Notice that there are more low than high cards (only 39 percent are high). Thus, early moves should be made with low cards when possible in order to conserve the highs. This fact causes many players to avoid even and odd in their secret patterns, because the cards are evenly divided in these two categories. But, of course, this tendency in itself can make the use of odd and even in the secret a surprisingly good idea.

In short, optimal strategy involves assessing the value of cards by the relative occurrences of their characteristics. Additionally, a player must consider the cards already showing on the table and in his hand in order to adjust the probabilities.

Opposite cards are often employed on successive turns to discover a particular element in a player's pattern. Thus the Six of diamonds (low, even, diamond) may be followed by the Jack of clubs (high, odd, club). If both are rejected, then either a heart or spade is called for. Be careful to save high cards in many cases and to let other players do much of the work in figuring out the various secret patterns in the game.

Finally, once the secret patterns are discovered, the game is still an exciting "efficiency" problem. This part of Secrets resembles a game called Fan-Tan, in which the deck is divided among the players, and the winner is again the one who first rids himself of all his cards. Clockwise play involves playing a card in the central pile or passing when no move is possible. In Fan-Tan, moves (discards) are allowed as follows: The Seven begins the play in any suit, after which a Six or Eight of that suit can be played, and then a Five or Nine, etc. A player cannot pass if a legitimate move is available. Thus each player knows at the outset what cards he will be using and their (presumed) relative values. The order of their play is the problem at hand. In this way, Fan-Tan resembles the final part of Secrets without the early puzzle-solving aspect. It differs from Secrets in that every card is potentially playable, while in Secrets (with the individual patterns chosen by the players) some cards can be useful while others are useless.

Variation: A variation that makes the game more interactive and more like others in this book requires each player to indicate (with a chip on the card perhaps) whether the card he just played on an opponent would have been acceptable to the corresponding element in his own secret. Otherwise all rules remain the same (subject to your imagination).

Sample card placement on table: Accepted (vertical) and rejected (horizontal) cards are displayed face up in front of each player. The deck is in the middle of the table.

CIRCUIT

Equipment: Circuit is played on a 5 by 8 grid. A checker board is a good playing field when three columns are covered. Checkers make fine playing pieces as well. Each player begins with one man in each of the five spaces of his home row.

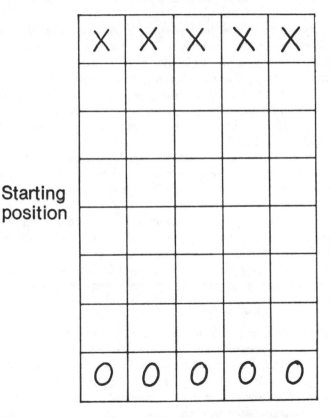

X's home row

Starting position

O's home row

Rules: Pieces can move one space in any direction, including, for example, diagonally backward. They can jump (capture) the opposition in any direction *except* diagonally. The player's home rows are "connected," in the sense that men may move from one home space "backward" to the corresponding (directly across) space in the other player's home row, if it is unoccupied. Thus it is as if the narrow ends of the board are attached, making the playing surface a cylinder. The exception to this cylindrical rule involves the corner spaces in one's home row. From these spaces, the option is to move to the *diagonally opposite* corner space of the other home row. Finally, a player cannot jump backward over his opponent's home row.

Object: To be the first player to advance *one* man safely "around" the board and back to one's home row. In other words, this piece must be moved a distance of *eight* steps.

Play: All "common sense" rules apply. Double jumps are allowed, jumps are not forced, and jumping a man in a given row counts as having passed through that row. A winner *must* traverse the board. He may not jump immediately to his opponent's home row and then jump back again to complete the circuit, although this is a completely legal series of moves. To avoid confusion, men that attempt to complete the circuit by immediately moving to the opposite home row and then making their way across the board should be "crowned" to identify their backward direction.

In short, there are two directions one can take to complete the circle and win the game. A player can immediately move to his opponent's home row and try to outrace his opponent back to his own home ground, or he can advance to his opponent's home row (while avoiding being jumped), which leaves him one move from victory.

Discussion: The pieces are used both offensively (by advancing toward the opposite home row and coming closer to circuiting themselves) and defensively (by restricting the spaces the opponent's pieces can move to—without being jumped) at the same time. In effect, the ability to simultaneously attack and defend increases the importance of each man and adds to the complexity of the game.

The illustration that follows shows the attack-defend combination and the foresight needed to make the correct move. Row 1 is X's home row. The asterisk indicates that a piece has been crowned.

	A	B	C	D	E
1	X			X	X
2		O	O		
3				X*	
4					
5			X		
6					
7			O		
8	O		O		

It is X's move. Up to this point, O's men in row 2 have been moving primarily as defensive men, trying to stop X.* (Note, of course, that in this example X cannot win by jumping his crowned piece from D3 to B1 because captures can *not* be made diagonally.) However, O now could win by moving C2 to B1, forcing X to jump from A1 to C1, thus allowing O to move B2 to A1 for a win on the following turn, A1 to E8. X can prevent all this by sacrificing his man with a move from D3 to D2. O must jump to prevent X from winning on the next turn (D2 to C1), and after X return jumps from E1 to E3, the game is wide open. The point of this example is simply that the role of both players' men can change between offensive and defensive very quickly, and a good player must be always aware of these possibilities.

Circuit places emphasis on the corner spaces because of the safety of the sides (corner pieces cannot be jumped) and the possible diagonal move to the opponent's home row. The value of the corners is not obvious to a beginner. Certainly one should try to make the opponent enter one's home board in one of the three middle spaces so that he can be attacked, but this is of paramount importance only when the opponent has come via the forward direction, through the middle six rows. If the opponent moves backward into one of your corner spaces then he can be more easily contained. Still, in most games, players will hold on to their corner spaces until confident of their strategy or until they need to take drastic measures.

This leads to the question of another general tactical decision: When, if ever, is it wise to send men backward? At first it seems that one should move to the opponent's home row as soon as a safe opportunity arises. Upon closer inspection, however, it becomes clear that an immediate move to one of the three middle spaces of the opponent's home row is not strategic, since the man can more easily be taken or forced to return to his own home row. A crowned man who must return to his starting row has gained nothing while the opposition is smirking, no doubt, and making constructive advances. Even the immediate move to a corner square is questionable, since a clever opponent will trap the man where he is. In some situations this can have its merits, however, because it will take at least two men to trap one man in the corner.

An early move to the opponent's home row is only useful to tie up a few of the opposition's pieces, and should not be tried if the man will immediately be forced to return. At later stages in the game, backward motion may be more useful both offensively and defensively.

Some end-game situations of Circuit can be readily analyzed when both players have depleted forces. When each player has just one man left, it's just a race; whoever has the lead will win. The same is true in a two-on-one situation, meaning that the single man will win if he has the lead.

If the end game is three-on-one, then the player with the three men left will always win, assuming that the single man still has to pass through the enemy home row, because two of the three can hold the man off while the third man eventually makes his way

around to home base. Even if the single man (O, let's say) has already made it past the opponent's home row and is moving backward toward his home base, X can still beat him if he has time to
send two men backward to form a line of defense in the row right
in front of O's home row (row 7 in the previous example). Setting
up the defense *in* the home row would be useless to X, because with
only two defensive pieces available, X could never block the three
home row spaces into which O could move to win (the space immediately in front of him, and those diagonally forward).

A three-on-two confrontation is much more complicated. Assume
at first that both players' men are moving forward. In order for the
shorthanded player to win, he must be far enough ahead in the
race to get both men in scoring position before his opponent's third
man can score. The reason for this is that even if O (the player
with two) has the man that is farthest advanced, he can be held off
by two of X's men. Thus it becomes a race between O's second man
and X's third man. This implies that O can begin the three-on-two
situation with both men closer to completing the circuit than any of
X's men and still lose because of the tremendous lead needed to advance both men to scoring position before X's one free man can
score.

The same thing is *not* true when one of O's two men is moving
backward and is the closest man to completing the circuit. Look at
the example on the following page.

Here O* is three spaces from completing the circuit, X is five spaces away (E4 to E8 to A1), and O is six spaces away. However, O's presence at B6 is enough to ensure a win for O. If O moves B6 to C7, X* must either jump, move, or be jumped, none of which is good. For example, suppose that X* moves D7 to E7. Then O* moves C5 to D6 and X cannot prevent a win by O. Or, suppose that X* jumps D7 to B7. Again O* cannot be stopped from reaching his home row. Finally, assume that X moves E4 to E5. O* then moves C5 to C6 and heads for victory.

To emphasize the importance of backward motion, recall the previous example of a three-on-two situation with no backward moving men. Suppose X has two men in the standard home row defense and a third man six spaces away from completing his circuit. If O has a man close to completing a circuit and another man still in his home row, previous analysis predicts a win for X, since his third man will beat O's second man to scoring position. A backward strategy can reverse this situation for O, however, since O's home row man can, if well placed, move directly to X's home row and effect a win for O by blocking for his comrade or by attacking X's defenders.

What can be concluded about the three-on-two end game? Clearly, if the player with three men has the man closest to completing the circuit he will win every time. In the case where the player with two men has the man who is winning the race, the eventual winner can only be determined after the player with three men has set up his two-man defense. At that point, the important elements are the number of spaces (in either direction) that O's second man must move before he can help O's first man (by occupying X's two defensemen), and the difference in the number of spaces to cover by O's closest man and X's closest man. In other words, if O's second man is three spaces away from being useful, and X's leading man is two spaces farther away from completing the circuit than is O's leading man, then X should win.

For more strategy discoveries, get out there and play Circuit yourselves. Enjoy!

TRIPLE-TAC-TOE

Equipment: Paper, pencil, and a little spare time. A 6 by 6 grid will do for a start.

Play: Three must play. Players proceed in turn (X, O, T) to occupy squares in the grid. The first 4row wins. If no player succeeds in forming a 4row, then the winner can be determined in a number of ways. The easiest version involves declaring the person with the most 3rows the winner. Another possibility is to declare it a draw and allow a different person to go first in the next game. The most interesting version is quite a switch: the player with the *fewest* 3rows wins!

Important Rule: Each variation is best played when each player is *required* to block an existing 3row if one is present at his turn. (The three need not necessarily be adjacent; for instance, O must block XX X as well as XXX). Thus if T forms a 3row, X may not move elsewhere and rely on O to block. In most cases, without this rule, the game will deteriorate into one player's choosing which of the other two will win. In the sample games that follow, X_1 is always the first move, O_2 the second, T_3 the third, and so forth. In this first game, the players have agreed that they will play according to the variation in which they draw if no one scores a 4row.

	A	B	C	D	E	F
1			X_{10}	X_{16}	T_{18}	
2			O_{17}	T_3	X_{19}	
3	O_8	X_7	X_1	X_4	T_6	
4	X_{13}	O_{11}	O_5	O_2	T_{12}	T_9
5			O_{14}			
6				T_{15}		

Notes to the sample game:

O_5: Allowing T (in T_6) to worry about X in row 3.

T_6: Better in E3 than B3 because now T_3–T_6 may be a threat.

X_7: Here X_7 is useful because it forces O to move away from O_5–O_2 in order to block X. O cannot ignore this and leave A3 to T_9 because the Important Rule forbids such behavior.

X_{19}: Required because of T_{18}–T_6–T_{12}.

When, in the absence of a 4row, the winner is the player with the *fewest* 3rows (ties share the pot), the strategic possibilities are increased as players try to force one another into forming 3rows. This next example illustrates this fine variation, after thirteen turns have been played. It is now O's turn.

	A	B	C	D	E	F
1						O_8
2			T_{12}		T_9	
3			X_1	O_2	X_7	
4			O_5	X_4	T_6	
5			O_{11}	T_3		
6		X_{10}		X_{13}		

Now O is about to be trapped. X will soon move into E6, for example, and according to the rules, O will be forced to block in C6, thereby forming the much detested 3row. T, of course, will assist X by staying away from row 6. O_{14} in E6 would not help because X can do the same damage by going to A6. O will suffer the 3row at O_{17}.

For a long time we adored this last version of Triple-Tac-Toe. There were many chances for collusion between two players when a series of games was played (for money, no doubt). The need for a three-person game and an unpredictable outcome was satisfied.

Now, however, we offer an even better game in the Tic-Tac-Toe family. Hidden-Tac-Toe as described on the following page will provide you with many hours of excitement. It can be played mindlessly (a doodling version) or carefully, with surprising results. Somehow this game is much better when each game involves a pot of a few cents per player (winner takes all).

HIDDEN-TAC-TOE

Equipment: Paper and pencil.

Object: To earn the most points. One point is awarded for each 3row, three points for each 4row. The game ends when there are just three empty spaces remaining or when no new mark has been placed for three consecutive moves.

Play: Three or four can play (or more with a bigger board). Players call out their moves all at once (perhaps at the count of three, like "One, two, three, shoot!"). The moves are then entered on the board. However, if on one move, two or more players seek to occupy the same space, these moves cancel one another and are not entered. Obviously, there is to be no discussion of moves, winking, or any other signaling beforehand.

This first illustration is of a 5 by 5 grid with three players: X, O, and T.

Boxes called out

Round	X	O	T	
1:	B2	B2	D3	X and O cancel out.
2:	C3	E4	C2	All moves okay.
3:	B4	E2	D2	All moves okay.

This configuration is *not* unusual. X hopes that O will try B1 to block T. T may sense that someone (or *both* X and O) will block in B1 and therefore will not try B1 himself. He hopes for a cancellation, which will leave B1 for later in the game. Remember that a successful T in B1 results in only 1 point, not an immediate victory.

Hidden-Tac-Toe can be played with four or five people in party fashion. One large board or sheet and a "recorder" (person) are all that's needed. Good luck!

HIDDEN THINGS AND FAREWELL

A recurring theme of the last two chapters of this book has been that the search for a "hidden element" can draw upon your puzzle-solving capabilities as well as your portfolio of gaming strategies. When you close this book you must remember to take with you the various themes that you have encountered in these pages and you must not hesitate to experiment with combinations of these motifs.

Now that you have had some experience with these themes you will continue to find that these patterns and strategies reappear in other games and puzzles—and, of course, in important everyday situations. We have already seen a variety of practical applications of contraction and expansion concepts. Similarly, we not only think of hiding our missiles from our enemies but also we consider moving them around (on tracks) in random fashion. Business competitors frequently try to uncover the nature and secrets of one another's price changes and product designs.

In short, the world is full of circumstantial puzzles. The tools and themes that have been developed in this book in the context of games and puzzles will be similarly applicable to countless other situations. As you search for more imaginative solutions to the problems you encounter, new themes will surface and, no doubt, they in turn will improve your arsenal of tools for working on still harder problems. Most of all, you will be a successful and innovative strategist if you take with you the realization that there do exist useful thematic approaches and if you continue to believe that there are new and better solutions out there waiting to be discovered.

ABOUT THE AUTHOR

Saul Levmore was born and raised in New York City, and received his undergraduate degree from Columbia. A Ph.D. in economics from Yale followed, and then a J.D., also from Yale. During his years at that University he designed and taught a seminar called "Construction and Analysis of Games and Puzzles." This book is, in part, an outgrowth of that seminar.

Mr. Levmore currently teaches law at the University of Virginia Law School.

Elizabeth Early Cook is a native of Old Saybrook, Connecticut, and received her undergraduate degree in history from Yale University. She now works as an insurance investigator in Cincinnati, Ohio, where she lives with her husband.